SINGLE PARENT

'When I left school I was ~~pregnant~~ and soon married.' So begins Maggie Durran's story. Six weeks after the baby was born, the marriage broke down. *Single Parent* is about the next twenty years – the pain, the heartache, and the hope.

This book offers real encouragement to parents who are struggling. With warmth and honesty Maggie Durran looks at the problems of single parenthood and shares her own experience of how a single parent family found its own identity.

Single Parent also gives practical advice on how and where to find help. It's a book for any lone parent, and for anyone concerned to help and understand an increasing number of families in society today.

To Jacqueline

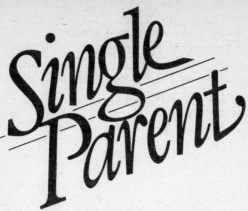

Single Parent

A PERSONAL STORY

Maggie Durran

A LION PAPERBACK
Tring · Belleville · Sydney

*With thanks to all the Durran family
and the Community of Celebration
who feature in this story.
Special thanks to Phyllis, my sister,
who typed the story for me
and remembered with me.*

Copyright © 1986 Maggie Durran

Published by
Lion Publishing plc
Icknield Way, Tring, Herts, England
ISBN 0 85648 848 8
Albatross Books Pty Ltd
PO Box 320, Sutherland, NSW 2232, Australia
ISBN 0 86760 806 4

First edition 1986

British Library Cataloguing in Publication Data
Single parent: a personal story.
   1. Single-parent family—Great Britain
   362.8′0941   HQ759.915
   ISBN 0 85648 848 8

Printed in Great Britain
by Cox & Wyman, Reading

CONTENTS

1

Single Parent

When I left school I was pregnant and soon married. With thirty pounds I had saved doing 'temp' work and a few wedding gifts we moved to Hackney, London.

My husband knew someone who had bought a sort of three-storey terraced house and was paying for it by renting out furnished rooms. We had a bedroom, twelve feet square, a kitchen about six feet square and shared a bathroom with all the other tenants. We moved in during November 1965. As the winter grew colder the landlord knocked a hole in the bathroom wall because the authorities had told him to install a washbasin. It was an enormous hole for a single waste pipe. And he didn't make any effort to stop the wind howling in. It was so cold.

As the damp on the bedroom wall turned to mould, the wallpaper began to fall off. I did buy a tiny Christmas tree and from somewhere we got a heater – perhaps from the landlord; I can't remember.

Jacqueline was born in Hackney General Hospital in a snowy spell in January. The hospital was warm and there was plenty of food.

My first few days as a parent were a jumble of feelings, highs and lows. More lows than highs. Having moved to London only a couple of months before her birth I knew practically nothing about pre- and post-natal care. When the nurses gave me instructions, I would stare uncomprehending, so they repeated themselves slowly and simply as if I were an idiot. I was a first-class example of the unprepared parent.

I was an unprepared mother. I was even more unprepared

for becoming 'father' as well as mother a few weeks later.

I do wonder why hospitals discharge people late on Saturday afternoons after the shops have closed. I managed to find a Jewish butcher's open on the Sunday. In the flat it was so cold I wore my coat.

When Jacqueline was a few days old and we were just home from the hospital there was a visitor. It was nine-thirty in the morning, the whole room was a disastrous mess, I was just about dressed, but my hair was unbrushed; Jacqueline was screaming and I was fraught. Then came the knock at the door.

'I am the Health Visitor. We call on all the new mums in our area to see how they are getting on.'

I stared back vacantly.

'I can see you are coping well, so I won't stop,' she said, and she went. She didn't come again. If she thought I was coping well, I dreaded to think how some of the other mums were doing!

Days were grinding and defeating – feeding times, nappy changes and endless laundry, which I dried on an airer in our bedroom. About eleven each morning I managed to go out to the shop or the launderette. We lived up two flights of stairs, so first I'd carry down the pram wheels, then Jacqueline in the carrycot, and lastly the shopping bags and laundry. Sometimes I repeated the process in the afternoon to walk the mile down to the Clinic.

At one level I was struggling desperately to believe I could even keep up with the needs of the baby. The marriage had already drifted into unreality. My whole time was consumed with staying alive, feeds, baths and trying to get warm. Emotionally I was very withdrawn, like some kind of zombie.

When Jacqueline was six weeks old we decided we wanted to move out of the city. At first I looked for a job to help pay for a house but then my husband decided to stay on alone in London and my job became earning a living for Jacqueline and me.

In those early days of Jacqueline's life the most basic pressure to find work outside the home was that we needed to eat, to be clothed and housed. I had to get a job. Even now, it is still very hard for me to realize that a new mother needs and often gets a lot of support and encouragement in the early months after the birth of a child – not so for me.

Jacqueline was seven weeks old when we moved out of London. I found a child-minder and began job-hunting. I was desperate enough to take any kind of work. I soon learned not to tell the whole truth.

In Leighton Buzzard there was an industrial area to the south of the town. Many of the factory units had moved from the London area, to newer brighter buildings that cost less. I trudged from factory to factory. A quite well-known manufacturer of expensive coats had one large unit on the estate. I went through the door hesitantly.

'Could I speak to the personnel manager, please?'

'Do sit down, I'll find out.'

As I sat there, I could see through into the factory area where cutting-out was going on. I had never seen anything more than home dressmaking. Here, layer upon layer of cloth was cut in one process, and each cut-out piece of a particular size was tipped into a bin, which was delivered to the machinists.

'Mr — will see you. Would you like to come upstairs?'

I jumped round, ready to follow the receptionist upstairs. The personnel manager was a reasonably friendly person, in his forties.

I went over with him my interest in finding a job. He then asked questions about me, my home circumstances, and my education. He made notes on a blue form. It was obvious that he was concerned that Jacqueline might be the cause of my being absent from work, but even more concerned about my education. More concerned, however, about what I had achieved than what I had not! He was quiet a moment.

'Oh yes, you could do the job and do it well. But if you are that well-educated you'll soon get bored and leave us, so we would have to train someone else. I suggest you look elsewhere.'

From then on I stopped telling interviewers about my qualifications unless they particularly stated that certain educational grades were needed.

I had not thought about parental roles when I became the only parent in our family. I have learned most of how to be a parent by being one and I have learned the roles by coming up against the problems of everyday life. Each of us learns something about identities, male and female, and ways of parenting from our own parents, and these we repeat. Growing up in a two-parent family helps show the span of responsibility but the single parent carries it all.

Having to be both the provider and the only parent I lived with the continual tension of doing two jobs. I wanted to care for Jacqueline at home and do the work of mother, not just trying to be housewife and mother in the evening. I wanted to be away from home the minimum number of hours. Against this was a near desperation at trying to earn sufficient to cover our expenses.

At that time we had digs with the person who looked after Jacqueline during the day. I fed her at six-thirty in the morning, got a bus at a quarter-to-eight and arrived home again at six. I sorted out bottles and food and laundry and a bottle for the night. She still woke at least once each night.

Once I started work, Jacqueline never again went to the Clinic for the kind of regular visits people make with babies. The Clinic was never open in the evening.

Eventually I found a job with a credit company, near the centre of town. Their offices, bright and clean, were above a car showroom. The company wanted clerks with higher educational qualifications to ensure that figures were copied correctly. So from 8.30 each morning I copied figures from ledger to ledger, payments made by people who bought on hire purchase. They were payments for cars bought in the showroom beneath the office. It was far more tedious than I imagined it was being a machinist in a coat factory. It was hard not to let tiredness overwhelm me as sums of money gradually filled the columns on the pages.

My life was a permanent financial disaster. I was sickened to find that the profit made by the company was in part made out of the people who couldn't manage to keep up the payments. I knew what it was like. I managed only very essential food and clothing, no luxuries. I felt indignant when I realized that employers tend to pay all eighteen-year-olds lower wages than older people. My sense of frustration arose from the fact that I had financial responsibility in the same way as older people, and yet I was earning so little.

What is coping? I remember Jacqueline's first smiles but I remember too the excruciating weariness. I needed to be on top of things but instead a creeping darkness was defeating me bit by bit. I was living on a tightrope but had very few balancing skills. I fell off when I got flu quite badly.

I phoned a message to my parents to see if they could help me out for the weekend. While I was there I told them I had discovered a house where I could rent a room. It would mean some shared facilities, but it was closer to my job and might save travel costs. I would need, however, to find a new child-minder or nursery to take Jacqueline. I was hopeful that I could.

My parents were appalled that we might move again to yet more squalid circumstances. And so, as it turned out, we stayed with them several years. My mother became the daytime 'child-minder'. She was determined that we should not go on living in one lot of digs after another. So, in practical terms, life became easier.

After such a brief episode of marriage I found myself back in the same old circles of friends.

'Oh, hello. I thought you were living in London. What are you doing here? Where's John,* is he around?'

'No, he isn't. It didn't work out, we've broken up.'

Silence for a few moments, then conversation picked up on local news, and so on.

It became obvious that male acquaintances did not think of me as married, although legally I still was. I got a few invitations.

'There's a party on Saturday. Would you like to come? I could pick you up.'

I thought that maybe I should try to embark on some kind of social life. It might help me to get over some of my shattered feelings. But I found that these men with whom John and I had been friends had only one thing in mind. Leave the party, stop the car in a gateway down some country lane and there ensued a rather sordid argument.

They always began, 'I really like you...' The whole scene made me feel sick. I rebuffed them but at the same time I felt like some strange kind of leper. Why was this happening? Why were these perfectly ordinary men behaving like this? I wondered if I was doing something to cause the situation.

One evening I found out.

'I'm fed up with this. What makes you think I want to?'

'It's just that you have been married. You must be used to sex and I thought you must miss it. So I thought...'

I felt sick, utterly sick.

None of these men saw how shaken I was, or if they did, they did not care. The trauma of my marriage had left

* Not his real name.

me with few inner resources for relationships and the last thing I wanted was to get involved in casual and unfeeling sexual relationships.

I dropped the whole circle of acquaintances.

When a marriage breaks down it affects your very sense of identity, of 'self'. I had been left with no self-esteem as a woman and there was inevitably a temptation to look for a replacement relationship, just to reassure me that I was acceptable. In other words, there was fairly considerable pressure to establish a new marriage. I was still married to John and by law at that time there was some while to go before I could ever get a divorce. So an invitation to a date was important but it was also a difficulty. In a funny kind of way it was a sign to me that I was still acceptable as a woman.

One day one of my old Rocker friends came round. He stayed and talked a while. Meeting Jacqueline he was delighted with her smiles.

'I heard you were married, then I heard you'd broken up. I am sorry.'

His words struck me as gentle and considerate. After that he came quite often. For six months he was a regular visitor and we often went out together. We were friends and he was glad to include Jacqueline in the company. He would have enjoyed being her father, and he used to try to come early enough to see her before her bedtime.

Yet all this time the turmoil was growing and exploding inside me. I would find myself staring into space and realize he was watching me.

'What are you thinking?'

There was no telling.

Sometimes I would start shaking with fear. I never managed to explain. I could never think how to tell anyone.

My sadness and my sense of despair grew. The friendship became a dilemma. Despite his concern and care and even love, we could never make the relationship he was looking for. He was understanding and caring but I could offer nothing in return. I had nothing to give and could find nothing in me to make another committed relationship. I could trust his commitment and faithfulness but I had only numbness where emotions ought to be. We parted sadly and without understanding enough to talk about the problem. It felt as if all the life in me had congealed into a solid rock inside me. I was stiff, hard, frozen.

2

Crisis Point

What were the prospects of finding another job? I certainly
needed more money than I was earning. I still had too little
for the most basic necessities. I did not even rent a television or have anything on hire purchase. I began to look
around.

A stationery manufacturer had newly moved from
Central London to the industrial estate in Aylesbury. The
money offered for a Sales Office job would more than com-
pensate for the cost of travelling. The interview went
reasonably well and I took the job offered, starting work
the following Monday.

The staff in the office all worked under considerable
pressure. High performance was essential to the work, or
the job itself was in jeopardy. I had thought I would be
good at the job but before long the pressure bred a great
sense of insecurity, and a feeling of stress. No mistakes
were tolerated.

My memories of that job are coloured by one or two
particular incidents. The open-plan office where I worked
was occupied by ten desks, each with a phone and a
constant stream of calls. The boss's desk was in one corner
where he could see what everyone was doing. Apart from
the modern design of the office, I felt like Bob Cratchett
working for Scrooge.

Every letter sent from the office had, apart from a copy
with the customer's original letter, another copy that went
in a file of daily correspondence. These were filed by date
and area of the country. We had to file our own letter copies
in a filing cabinet in the corner of the office. Just a few

weeks into the new job I went to put away some copies. I grabbed the file drawer which, to my horror, slid right out with a resounding crash, strewing its thousand letters across the floor.

There was a deathly hush. All the other clerks looked over to me in terror. No one moved. Feeling the boss's thunderous glare, I restored the offending drawer and began to gather the paper. It took ages to re-file the whole lot. I expected to be sacked, but was not.

All the time I was there I was one hundred per cent unhappy. I was filled with an overbearing sense of darkness. Dread was draining me of energy and the ability to think. I followed a rigid routine, seeming to put one foot in front of the other in a repetitive motion, yet I always felt too vulnerable, quite lost.

I was terrified of losing Jacqueline. At the same time I thought myself meaningless to her. The darkness was closing in on me. Only the routine kept me going. I went automatically from one action to the other. No looking out or up, just one step more into the darkness.

The mildest unexpected action or movement threw me into such stress I was shaking. One evening a neighbour knocked on the back door, arriving for a typing lesson with my sister. I was drying Jacqueline from her bath and was so startled that she began to cry. Another time I was on my way home from work when I saw an ambulance with a flashing light. Immediately I burst into tears, convinced that Jacqueline was being carried away, critically injured, to the hospital. A week or so later fear made me stop riding my scooter altogether and I would only travel by bus.

The horror movie that was inside me began to impinge on the outside. I could no longer tell what was real. I began to fear strange faces that whispered and peered in the windows at night. I was terrorized by the creatures that crawled in a writhing mass over the bedroom floor in the darkness. I could not get up to Jacqueline in the night unless I had the light on – that made the creatures scuttle back under the skirting-boards.

It was a terrifying nightmare that pervaded all my senses day and night. I tasted and smelled the horror which filled me totally.

I told no one.

They would, I was sure, clap me away in some madhouse.

In December 1966, when Jacqueline was eleven months old, I saw one of those documentaries on television that are intended to stop people drinking and driving, by frightening them. It finished me off. I tried to speak to someone who didn't know what I was saying. I was trying to bridge that monumental gap between the ordinary talk of everyday life and the shadowy ghosts who were eating me alive.

I withdrew and went to bed. Under the weight of the covers and surrounded by my nightmares, I planned my own death. There was no possible escape from my circumstances or the oppression that surrounded me. There was no way for me to cope. I decided to die and began to plan my exodus from life.

That night I reached only a firm decision to do it. The next night I considered the method. In my teenage days I had thought that life beyond the age of thirty was unbearable. I had planned to spend my thirtieth birthday riding the fastest motorbike at the hardest wall I could find. Whatever I chose now, it had to be foolproof, instantaneous. I wanted no more pain.

Sometime in the small hours of the night I looked forward to the soft oblivion of endless dark. Then my whole skin crept as I recollected that it might not be the end. What if there were really an eternity and eternal pain, on and on and on? I could only kill myself if my consciousness were going to be destroyed by death. My despair was hysterical.

11

'God, if you are there, you have got to help me.'

At that moment, I think someone started sweeping up my darkness with a dustpan and brush and emptying it into the bin.

From then on circumstances began to change around me, while I was passive among them. The first thing was finding a new job.

I had worked in the Sales Office job for nearly a year. One of the pressures in that busy office was the boss, whose chief interest seemed to be in putting down his staff. Criticism and derogatory remarks abounded. I had dared not leave, for at least I got a reasonable wage there and it had never occurred to me to complain to the management.

The day I handed in my notice the Sales Director summoned me to his office. It was a modern new open-plan building with ferns and a wide hallway. The directors were all upstairs. I went up and knocked timidly at his door.

'Why are you leaving?'

'My new job is nearer home and there is more pay.'

For the first time my wages would cover my expenses.

'Have you enjoyed working here?'

Well, what should I say? I could have told him anything I liked. In fact, I told him what I had experienced.

'I am tired of being belittled. The Sales Manager always wants to cut everyone down. I would have left sooner if I could have found another job.'

'Why did you not come and tell me before?'

I shrugged. 'What good would it do?'

'A lot. We could have changed it.'

I heard later that the man had been sacked. Other employees had left the company for similar reasons to mine.

What struck me, however, was that someone *cared*. I suppose other people may have done too but this was the only one that I met, and I couldn't believe that anyone could be bothered about whether I was unhappy at work.

Once I began to work for the Civil Service the pressures changed. As long as you did not do anything drastically wrong, like break the Official Secrets Act or steal or do nothing, it seemed that a Civil Service job was secure, with a good pay scale. The new job brought higher pay and I managed to make ends meet. My sister worked at the same place so I went with her in her car, no need to use the scooter.

The high stress factor in being the provider decreased. I found I had not lost Jacqueline by having her looked after all day by someone else. Each morning when I left she would wave goodbye and from mid-afternoon she would keep running to the gate to see if I was coming home. While I hated leaving her, it was obvious she wanted to be with me even more than I wanted to be with her. This reassured my fears that she would look to the child-minder as 'mother', not me. I was glad Jacqueline missed me when I was not there. I was definitely still her mother and, regardless of all the trauma and insecurity, that never changed.

The job itself required me to be methodical but relatively brainless, simple sums really, entering figures into the right columns and balancing them once a month. The days came and went less oppressively. It was a workplace with more social life, a little more friendly.

I managed quite often to carry a semi-relevant piece of paper to someone else's office and then to chat to them for a while. We had lunch at the pub and everyone laughed a lot. Mind you, the tea was really bad and I used to get stomach-ache from it.

Later in the year my sister changed jobs, so I began to ride the scooter again and Jacqueline began to talk.

My parents had given me a hand-driven sewing machine for a wedding present. I put it to good use. I made lots of Jacqueline's clothes, looking through remnant stalls for

13

suitable sale-price materials. One lunchtime I found some wonderful cotton fabric that had little children in its design. It was lovely, not like the garish designs I saw in so many 'nursery' prints. I made Jacqueline lots of smock dresses of this and other materials.

The step I had taken of moving in with my parents had helped. While it is often incredibly difficult to share a house with other adults it can be easier with parents. There are at least some similarities in approaches to family life and values, though it is important to establish who is deciding how the children are raised, the questions of discipline and sweets between meals, hours of TV watching and other standards.

I gave my mother a contribution towards the house-keeping costs. I hung on to enough to pay for transport and lunches at work and little else. Yet what I paid into the household budget was not a fair proportion of the cost of rent, rates and heat. Nor did it pay my mother for being the daytime child-minder and occasional baby-sitter. As I had no more money, it was probably the only way I could have survived.

There was the question of maintenance money. It took time and effort to be awarded it, yet even then it was not guaranteed, nor was it sufficient to support our family. I had seen my husband only a couple of times after he had decided to stay in London and he had given me a little money then. My impression is that he thought I was earning enough for our keep, that we were again single people without commitments to one another. I couldn't find a way to begin to talk about the problem and I felt guilty about not earning enough myself.

It was the question of custody that brought me to court the first time. When I heard that John was living with another woman and wanted to have Jacqueline with him, I was terrified. I had never seen a solicitor in my life before, and I only found one at the suggestion of family friends.

14

Otherwise, I would have had no idea about how or where to start.

At lunchtime I left work, walked into town, into the reception of a solicitor's office and asked for an appointment.

It was a tremendous relief when I heard that there was no question that anyone else might have legal custody of Jacqueline. I was told that the mother always got custody of young children unless she was proven unfit. Older children, over seven, are the subject of more discussion before a decision is made, and are even given the choice sometimes.

I heaved an enormous sigh of relief. Then the solicitor had a question for me: Was I getting money from my husband regularly to support Jacqueline and myself? He advised that we take the case to court to get a fair maintenance payment.

What did that mean? Wouldn't I have to pay? After all, I had no money.

Again, I was reassured. Legal Aid would pay for the case. 'Legal Aid' meant that money would be paid by the State on my behalf. The solicitor would be paid by Legal Aid, then they would send me a bill, allowing me to pay them back over a number of months.

The case came up in a tiny, village Magistrates' Court, straight after a case about a minor traffic offence. Since my case involved a child, the court was cleared of anyone not directly involved. It was held *in camera*, in order to protect children. My custody of Jacqueline was confirmed, and I was awarded maintenance totalling four pounds a week.

For a while I received that much, though I was sure that it was hard for my husband to find it out of his wages and still live! A year later, I returned to court as the payments had stopped and he was told to pay the original amount and gradually pay off the arrears.

I returned to court because of my need. I disliked being dependent in any way on someone who wanted nothing to do with Jacqueline and me; he had long since stopped visiting. I wanted a complete break but was unable to make it because I found no other means of financial help. It was not vengeance but poverty!

I had enough money to pay the Legal Aid bill immediately. After that, I was glad when the money came but, once I was really earning enough to manage on, I gave up trying to get payments. I do not think continued court cases would have changed the situation.

I came across no organizations that would help me in my situation. There was one organization I heard of through women's magazines that helped single mums but it seemed to spend its time getting babies into adoption rather than helping the family cope with life as it was.

I know I would never under any circumstances have had Jacqueline adopted by anyone else, even if it might have helped in some of the particular practical problems we had. Where I needed help was to make life work for us, given our circumstances.

From the financial point of view, there had been no other course than the one I had taken – of getting a job immediately. At the time I was unaware of any scheme that would have helped me find housing, though I had heard of one organization that temporarily housed unmarried mothers and their children.

The crisis nature of my job-hunting meant I was initially looking for anything that would bring in some money. Later, when I got the Civil Service job, life became less crisis-bound. It was good to have a job that was not likely to end soon, not seasonal or temporary. It was a friendly place, sympathetic to my being a mother. I had experienced those places which thought of me as potentially unreliable, because I might possibly be called away if Jacqueline was sick. In an emergency I needed whoever was looking after

Jacqueline to be able to contact me without that going against me in the job.

Would Jacqueline have been better off with two adopted parents who had more money and more stability? After all, she was only six weeks old when her father left, she would not really have known that her parents were changing. For me it was worth all the work, the fight to make ends meet. For we were inseparable, we belonged to one another. I could only consider life in terms of the two of us together. We were not two separate individuals whose lives might be considered independently. We did not exist independently – however impoverished, emotionally or financially, we were a family.

3

Finding a Future

Even after the years of raising four lively children of his own, my father had lots of love for his grandchildren. Each had a special place in his heart. From the time Jacqueline began to smile at him he always made time for her. We – my parents, sisters, brother and I – are a family that help one another without question. None of us has ever had much money, but we have always been ready to help one another with whatever we do have.

Through that November and December my father spent lots of evenings in the shed. Since he had already done a long day's work we wondered what he was up to. He would not tell us, just came in from time to time to warm his hands round a cup of tea. It was Christmas before we found out. There was a very large parcel awaiting Jacqueline's attention.

'For me?'

'You open it. It's a present for you.'

He was a bit shy about it. She was not sure what to do, so he helped tear off the wrapping. Inside was a wooden horse on wheels. It had a neatly padded seat and she could sit on it to be pushed along, or push it along herself. It was a very straight upright horse with a string mane and no tail. Over the next two summers whenever Dad or anyone else mowed the lawn Jacqueline ran up and down with her horse, helping. Peter Teddy used to ride in the space on the wooden base under the horse's body.

My father wanted to tell her stories, take her with him on whatever he was doing, whether working on his allotment or delivering papers. She learned to plant seeds in the garden and potatoes on the allotment – 'two steps and another potato'. At harvesting time she picked up potatoes in her seaside bucket and tipped them into the sack just as we all did. He bought her a comic on Saturdays and she sat on his knee while they read it together.

During the day Jacqueline ran around after my mother. With the aid of a child-sized dustpan and brush from the market, she helped around the house. She loved being in the garden and learned lots about flowers. Together they visited some of the neighbours and sometimes Jacqueline went out to visit one or two of them on her own, to have a cup of tea and hear them talk about times long ago when they were children.

Our house was near the end of a row of council houses ending at the village green. The road ran north with several houses to the west, some cottages and the local pub. To the east, the green sloped downwards to a small brook on Duck Lane. Here several farms looked west across the green. Jacqueline used to follow a footpath from our house down the slope of the green, over a footbridge and into Duck Lane. She turned right and twenty yards further on the left was Mrs Hawthorn's home, Brook Cottage.

Jacqueline loved to visit Mrs Hawthorn. She liked the old dark furniture, the photos and the Victoriana. There were pretty china cups and antique chairs and every piece seemed to have a story. And Mrs Hawthorn's stories were of long-ago days that were real, not just stories from books.

It was a good environment for Jacqueline. A series of child-minders and bedsits and nursery school would not have given her this kind of life. I do not know if there were more possibilities open to us, I had no way of finding out.

At that time I met another of those friendly people who helped for no apparent reason. Dick had been a teacher at the school where my sister had gone. He told us stories of being afraid of her, remembering the day he had marked her book wrong when the work was in fact correct. He had withered under her stare.

Dick was now teaching in further education.

One day he asked me about my education. I told him.

'Then *what* are you doing here?' he asked.

'I'm all right. I might get promoted, then I'll get more money.'

'But this – for the rest of your life? You must be joking!'

I explained my circumstances.

'So what! You must be able to get something better.'

A few days later he brought up the subject again. 'I've got an idea.'

I looked up, surprised.

'You could teach.'

'I couldn't. It would mean going to college and they would hardly have Jacqueline in a students' hall of residence.'

'I doubt if they would. But it may not be impossible. Now listen, I have a friend who is the bursar of a college. It's not too far from here. We could find out what he suggests.' He could tell I thought there was not much hope. 'Okay, I'll write to him and ask for the information for you.'

The fellow with the dustpan really did seem busy, taking action to get my life sorted out.

Dick turned up with an application form.

'Fill this in.'

'I can't.'

'You can. You can't just vegetate in this place for the rest of your life.'

My sister Phyllis took a day off and drove me to the interview at the college. It seemed as if the interviewer was quite opposed to people in my circumstances – it was all she talked about. I found out that the college took day students, but I decided I would not go even if I was offered a place; I was not going to face that kind of supercilious criticism for the next three years.

Dick was equally adamant.

'Look, we have got this far. You must not give up now. The person who interviewed you is leaving this year. You won't ever meet her again.'

Two days later a letter came offering me a place. Although it was only a matter of months since the night of my despair I had a strong suspicion that I was being helped, through the people I met.

The possibility of becoming a teacher held a very high attraction for me as a working parent. I realized that by the time Jacqueline reached school age I would be working in a job which shared the same holidays. My working day would also be similar to hers. Evening marking and preparing could be done at home. I could see the potential for an easing of the tension between work and home.

The question of a grant came up. I decided that what I was offered would finally determine whether or not I could go to college. In the event, it was as high as my salary had been, so I went.

I seemed to have inched my way out of a pothole. Some people talk of Christian religious conversion as a blinding flash or a sudden realization. I had none of these. But my daily experience, my circumstances and the way in which they changed, showed me that something purposeful was happening. I could only relate it to my desperate prayer in the darkness – this steady opening up of life before me. The Civil Service job had been one such step and the grant another. It did appear that someone was carefully and considerately opening doors for me and enabling me to step forward.

As a child I had skipped along, experiencing life coming to me like a stream, gurgling and splashing or dawdling dreamily, bringing good and indifferent days. As an adult I realized that while this stream keeps coming and can never stop, much can be made of it. Bridges and tunnels, dams and waterfalls. I can do something with it.

Being married had happened to me and disappeared again without my having any consciousness of myself within it. This perspective remained unchanged till after I became aware of God's love and purpose. Once I had experienced not simply an inner subjective 'feeling' but the real activity of God in the circumstances of my life, I became aware not just of the source of the stream but of the possibility of directing and harnessing the stream of life within me, my potential.

What was it that made me realize that the person, Maggie Durran, had some untapped potential and that, however limited the choices, I could do more and better? It was the beginnings of self-esteem. I recollect that as a child I had had good expectations; as a teenager I had few. Now as a young adult I had found myself with a little potential that I could choose to develop. That seemed good.

My first memory of this growing awareness that there was more to life than what I was doing then was with Dick. As he talked to me about college, he had said, 'This kind of job that you have now, you can do easily. It's regular money, it's reliable. That's fine if you are near retirement or feeling old. But you are not, you have your whole life ahead of you. You could make something of it. What about doing something that you could enjoy and grow in?'

His view of life was expansive. I felt bigger on the inside. Maybe there could be new horizons, new choices – it was a ray of hope.

My middle-of-the-night appeal to God had brought me experiences that led me to new possibilities. Until that moment life had been only a tunnel to death, to be endured. It had been like one of those gigantic hoppers at the cement factory. Great rocks were carted in by the lorryload from the quarries and then tipped down the chute to the hopper. At the bottom were enormous steel teeth that chomped and chewed the rocks into small stones. Then another different set of teeth ground and rolled them

22

to powder. After that, water turned it to slurry and finally it came out as fine dust, indistinct and shapeless. It had felt as though I was the rock and life was the process that chewed and ground me to dust. I had felt powerless against its force.

Now life was like rolling up a huge snowball. As I experienced more of life I was getting bigger, not being diminished. To get back to my earlier illustration, this is the stream of life, given by God – I can enjoy it and can develop my potential right in the middle of the stream.

At the same time as this awakening, I was trying to establish myself socially – in the village, and – later – at college.

I was rushing out of the house one day when the Rector came up to the door.

'Oh, you must be Margaret. I've met the rest of the family. How nice to meet you.'

'Hello.' I neither knew him nor did I care very much at the time. Much later we made friends with all of his family.

'I would like to say how nice it would be to see you in church one Sunday.'

My thoughts were not that nice. I was only too aware of the 'tut-tut's' of other people seeing a nineteen-year-old alone with a child. I was tired of moralizing superior attitudes. He went on, 'We really don't judge you for what has happened. We don't think badly of you for it.' I don't think he did.

In fact, I did go to church once that year. But the God I was experiencing did not seem to fit their ways of talking and worshipping. I got as far as 'Our Father' in the Lord's prayer and stopped. The words of that prayer and the rest of the service were depressingly futile, meaningless. I had so little in common with those people, so I did not go again for a long time.

But I was changing and finding that I had not a lot in

23

common with my old friends, either. In my teenage years on motorbikes I had gone out for a few weeks with a boy who had one of the best bikes around. He was very quiet, almost shy. Now he turned up, in a car, to see me. I hardly recognized him without the helmet and goggles! One thing about Rockers was that whatever you started out looking like, the faster you travelled the more your eyes ran and the less your hair looked as if it had ever had any style. You had to be a Rocker to appreciate other Rockers.

Well, here he was with a suit and tie, the lot. He was a bit embarrassed. 'Would you like to come out for a drink?'

The pub we went to was a few miles away. There was a disco in a back room, with strobe lights. It was an update of the places we used to haunt. He tried valiantly to start up conversation, several times. I could think of absolutely nothing to say. In the end, we exchanged only a few sentences. Our worlds were now too far apart. He took me home.

'Well, that wasn't much good, was it? I thought I would like to go out with you again but it would never work.' Off he went. We now had almost nothing in common. The distance that experience and time had put between us was immense.

During these days I was still, however unconsciously, trying to find some self-esteem as a woman. For a year or so, including part of my first year of college, I went out fairly regularly with someone who was quite different. He was a thinker and a lot of our time we spent talking. I was trying to come to terms with my growing awareness of God. He was inquisitive without being controlling, and was interested in the way I thought and felt about life and its meaning. He was always lending me books.

One evening we were in a pub in the Bicester area. It had looked nice as we passed, so we had turned back to go there. Having got our drinks, we sat down at one of the four small tables. It was midweek and the pub was empty. A couple in tweeds came and stood at the bar to drink, the husband was a well-to-do farmer type, who lounged comfortably, chatting to the landlord.

Then another couple came to one of the tables. She spoke in a high-pitched, over-loud voice, sort of dominating. As the conversation continued it seemed she was a helicopter pilot. He was obviously in the Forces, and their conversation got louder and more insistent, more competitive. It was like watching a hard-fought tennis match. She was insecure in her identity, despite her skill, and he obviously could not cope with women who were equals. My friend and I got more drinks. An hour or so later we left there, only to realize we had never spoken a word, apart from ordering drinks. It wasn't like us at all! We laughed all the way to the car. It made me realize how much we were able to listen to each other without being threatened by the other's identity.

He used to ask me about the things I read. More interesting often than the books themselves, was my response to what they said. I was beginning to find out what I could, or could not, agree with. I was getting to know myself, to know what I thought and why I thought it.

Although I was gradually coming to feel better about myself as a woman, I wanted more. My feelings about myself were conflicting, and hence confusing. Deep down I felt extremely guilty about my marriage – I had been wrong and inadequate, I was sure. I was craving a response from others that would tell me I was all right, that I was acceptable, physically and as a whole person. All this was unspoken. Friendship was helpful, but my inner programming was always checking on whether this proved I was all right or not. So most romantic relationships were highly pressured for me – was I *really* all right? The ordinary friendships, the hardly-noticed ones, were in fact the more helpful, the more affirming.

I was plodding uphill, to re-establish a sense of self-esteem and self-worth. At times I felt hardly more than a shadow. I was surprised to be noticed, or remembered or included. At the same time, too, I was a parent. I plodded away intuitively at what to do. I hope that where a family has two parents they affirm and encourage one another as parents, and as people.

4

Finding Myself

In the early days of my time at college Jacqueline was still tiny and it was hard to do anything more than simply work and sleep each twenty-four hours. I found myself in a day students' class with a timetable carefully designed for mothers to get home to schoolchildren at 3.30p.m. Resident students finished later. Most of the day students were mature women, their children at school. I was younger and alone. The pressures they experienced were hard but different from mine. They had to find time to be with a spouse, with children, do housework and homework. What we did have in common was the rush to leave college at the end of the afternoon and our home-life was already so busy there was little time to make friends with each other.

As the course progressed, however, into the second year, I met other students. As we began to specialize in our particular chosen subjects, the groups became more mixed. I made more contacts among those students my own age. I was twenty-one.

After a while some of the students who lived in at the college invited Jacqueline and me to visit at weekends. She enjoyed riding the stone lions in the quadrangle and liked to sit there watching people go to and fro.

Being accepted at college was a sign to me that I really could become more than I was then. I realized that the ups and downs of life were not signs of the gnashing teeth in the cement hopper, but signs of being human. Human life includes setbacks and failures, these are episodes of life. Believing in life and in myself helped me to grow, to see each challenge as a stage to the next.

In my first year of college I studied all subjects as the training was for teachers at Primary levels. We looked at all aspects of the syllabus. I did quite well in many subjects and found myself with several possible specializations at the end of that year.

The religious education syllabus was organized and taught by someone who reminded me of the teacher I had had at school – maybe that was why I got so frustrated at the way religion was taught. It seemed to bear no relation to real experience. Yet at the end of that year I knew that the God who had answered my prayer, who was sweeping up the darkness, was the one the Christians talked about. I did not like the way they talked, or even how they practised their religion – but it was the same God.

I drifted closer to the church, but could not find a denomination that suited me. The local evangelical Anglicans were very nice people, but not quite what I wanted. I went to a Baptist church in a nearby town. They all knew each other well and I never felt I could fit in. Eventually, I chose a city-centre church where no one knew anyone, so at least I was not different. Not too different that is, though eventually I got the impression that children were not welcome. I got some hard stares when Jacqueline, who was really very quiet, dropped her crayon or rustled the pages of her book. The stewards told me several times about where the crêche was held but I wanted Jacqueline with me – we already spent too much time apart. So she stayed.

The anonymity suited me, gave me space.

Jacqueline and I drifted in and out of several groups of people. In an environment where a key to social activity was gradually to form couples, I was at a distinct disadvantage. One or two hopeful men approached, only to retreat, shocked that I was married with a child yet present in a group of single students.

I let the situations drift by, and took in what I could use. As a beginner Christian I took little notice of what was negative and found much that helped. I still had great bouts of darkness, covering them up by working very hard, so that I could ignore them. They have grown less over the years, but never totally disappeared. It was hardest when such times as teaching practice came. Then my fears of failure, often irrational, made me work far harder than I would have done otherwise. I dared not fail in any way.

There were some good friends. Maggie was a single student, resident in college, whom I got to know quite well. We met in a history tutorial, discussing some aspect of England under the Tudors. In some ways we were very different. She was always neat and particular – I still am not. Yet we got along well. Maggie came with me to the divorce court in the autumn of 1969.

I had waited for what was then the statutory three years to pass before I could apply for a divorce on the grounds of desertion. I saw my solicitor, paid out all my savings and quite quickly got a date to go to court.

There was no Legal Aid help in applying for a divorce. I had to pay out a hundred pounds, hope I was awarded costs and then that my husband would pay. As it happened, he eventually did.

I had asked Maggie if she would go with me, as I was extremely nervous and wanted someone to talk to to ease the pressure.

At that time I owned a car, so I picked Maggie up at college and we drove to Northampton. Arriving at the court we found three other divorce cases set for that day; they were being taken in alphabetical order. We sat in the court listening as the other three were dealt with.

I was going hot and cold, my mouth was dry – all the signs of stress. Above all, I did not want to see my husband. I hoped desperately that he would not come. The other three cases passed in twenty-five minutes. It would soon be over.

My turn came. I was only vaguely aware of some official saying to the judge that my husband was coming but had not arrived. The judge called a ten-minute break. I watched the clock hands creep round. I was shrivelling up inside.

My case was called. I had to go into the witness stand and swear to tell the truth. As I opened my mouth to answer one of the first questions my husband walked in. I was afraid both of my feelings and that he would cause some kind of scene or argument of which I would be ashamed, in which I would be crushed again. I am sure my face must have expressed my fears, for the judge repeated the question and was very gentle with the questions that followed.

When had my husband left me? How had I managed financially? What were the custody arrangements and what maintenance was awarded? Did I regularly receive the maintenance money? Who looked after Jacqueline during the day and what were my plans for the future? He spent most time on these last two aspects, showing, as I had seen in the previous cases, considerable concern about children and their welfare.

My husband was called out but was allowed very little time – not sufficient, I thought, to warrant a trip from London. I was surprised that he had come since he contested nothing, but he did seem to want to explain his actions. I was granted the divorce and awarded costs which were eventually paid to me – the return of my savings. But that was the last money I ever received.

'What now?' asked Maggie afterwards.

'I want to get out of here as fast as I can. I don't want to talk to John, so let's go.' John was talking to a court official – I thought he was arguing – as we left. We ran along the street and down a side-street to the car. I could barely drive for the stress I was feeling.

Another good friend at that time was Michael, studying

theology as a second degree. When college broke up for the vacation I was on my own again, until I found that Michael, whose home was abroad, was still around. We spent many evenings talking in his college room. I think I learned from Michael to begin to make some order out of my experience of God. He explained lots of traditions to me and I suppose I gained my first understanding of theology. We talked endlessly about politics and life in general. It was he who gave Jacqueline a shell from Africa – a very large conch – in which she heard the sea. It came in a small African basket with a lid and a long string handle. For years he was 'Michael-who-gave-me-the-African-basket'. His friendship gave me room to be myself.

Becoming a Christian was what I suppose had happened. I would describe it as finding God – when I had reached the end of living. The reality of what I experienced, the way circumstances changed and the care and love of a variety of people brought me a renewed reality. Many of those who helped me by opening up significant doors did not do so with any conscious effort – yet the sum of all that I experienced was an overwhelming realization of God's love.

I was never convinced by fine preaching. Even now, while I can recognize a good preacher, I am more convinced by what I experience. The preaching and teaching can only confirm and give perspective to my experience.

Probably few of my student acquaintances knew that I was a single parent, but I began to find a closer circle among them. I certainly realized that I could be 'categorized' as unusual, when they got to know Jacqueline. But I experienced few negative responses among many positive ones.

I found it hard to sort out for myself the standard Christian teaching on marriage. A much-respected couple, for instance, spoke at a meeting about marriage being the coming together of two halves, who become complete together! I did not feel like half a person yet, according to these people, I was. Could they be right? If God had, as they said, chosen another half for each of us, and we had only to be patient till we met, I had got problems. There was no way I could fit this model now. Neither did I see myself as a sort of half-person – one arm, one leg, one eye, and so on. I was trying to be two people, really, with all I had on my plate. No, their model did not fit life.

The fact that I was peculiar did not seem to mar the friendships I made then. Jacqueline and I began to meet these friends at church on Sundays and we all enjoyed the picnics and punting that were part of student life in the summer. I eventually adopted the pattern of work that many of the others followed, working Monday to Saturday on my studies and having Sunday as a break. As I was always worried about whether I would get all the work done as well as I wanted to, this helped me take some necessary time off.

One Sunday as we lazed in the sun, Jacqueline found a load of grass cuttings to play in. A few minutes later she had covered my friend Jonathan in heaps of grass: they had fun together. Another evening Tom invited her to his college to try blowing his trombone. She managed a sort of snort and lots of giggles.

There were some possibilities that were too difficult for me to take up because of being a mother as well as a student. For example, some students stayed on an extra year to take the degree course in Education. I was offered a place on the course but found I could not maintain home life and studying, with the extra work involved.

Sometimes the normal schedule was almost too much for me. At Easter 1970, I was heading up to final exams. I kept up all the set work and teaching practice and began to revise. I was used by now to my routine of leaving home for college at around eight-thirty and arriving home at four or four-thirty. I spent my time with Jacqueline till after her bedtime, then began my college work at eight, or later. I seldom finished before midnight. Often I worked till one or two in the morning. It was a fine balance that got upset only a few weeks before my final exams. I caught flu, then Jacqueline got a bug that had me up with her several nights. The pressure was almost too great.

Alan, a post-graduate friend, had invited us to tea. We went, feeling tired, but glad to get out of the house. He took one look at me.

'Goodness! What has happened to you? Sit down.'

'What do you mean?' I asked, sitting on the armchair by the window.

'You look awful; are you ill?'

'I have had flu, but I'm getting better now.'

'How much work are you doing? Don't you need a break?'

'I daren't stop now. There's just too much still to do.'

Jacqueline was sitting in the window-seat, swinging her feet and staring out into the garden.

'And Jacqueline has been ill so we have lost some sleep. But she is better now.'

'But you cannot work like that, it's too much strain. This may sound grim but I've known friends working too hard who have had a breakdown right before finals. And I don't want you to.'

I was nearly in tears by this point.

'I think you should stop working. You won't fail now. You've worked hard and you know your stuff. I don't mind helping you work out a schedule that is realistic.'

I do not often tolerate bossy people, yet Alan was not normally bossy. He was just the kind of friend I needed at the time. From then on I hardly worked in the evenings at all until the weekend before exams. I was in such a habit of pushing myself that I had not seen how near the brink I was. If I hadn't had the break, I would have failed through trying too hard.

Student life and friendships are perhaps somewhat special. I left college and went into the real world of ordinary working life again. The college environment had brought together enough people for there to be a circle of Christians who had much in common. When I started teaching, I moved to a new area, away from family and friends, as well as from student life.

5

A New Start

By the time I left college and started teaching I had gone
through a personal reformation. From the hopelessness
and powerlessness of my despair I had surfaced beyond
the tunnel with a sense of purpose in life. I felt a tentative
freedom and determination to be myself. I had sufficient
experience of God to know I was going to live by trusting
in him. I was beginning to live.

Another new start.

For a while I had thought of buying a house. I liked
the idea of the security it would bring and was even
interested in a little cottage I saw every day on the way
to college. But I realized that I could never have got a
mortgage – money was too scarce. I have never owned a
house and probably never will.

I started to look for rented accommodation. My impression of council accommodation was that only the most
needy cases reached the top of the waiting-list so I didn't
apply.

In the village where I started teaching, I found a privately-
owned house to rent – a little cottage in a side-street where
we found lots of good neighbours. The house had two
bedrooms upstairs with the living-room, kitchen and
bathroom downstairs. It took a while to gather enough furniture. I bought a cooker on hire purchase but apart from
that we had what we could collect. Rob, my brother-in-
law, came across a three-piece suite that was being thrown
away – once re-covered it was excellent. My aunts gave
me a folding guest bed that I used for myself and my
parents gave us a chest of drawers and a few other

pieces they no longer needed. During the winter we bought two electric heaters but for economy we tried to use the coal fire in the living-room most of the time.

I was teaching Maths at a comprehensive school, and Jacqueline started at the primary school next to it. We were doing almost the same hours. It was a small village with children coming by coach from up to ten miles away to the school. Most of the teaching staff lived in the towns around, travelling by car each day, so I had little other than working contact with them. In this new situation Jacqueline and I were very much alone again. We had moved away from my parents who had helped us so much; we were now slightly nearer my older sister. But visits to the family and to other friends were expensive – in time, not to mention money, given our budget.

Sometimes I felt very poor; sometimes we were.

One day I called into the office of the local Magistrates' Court to collect my maintenance but still there was none. At that time I had too little petrol in the car and no money. I found a jewellers shop that would buy my wedding ring – the man said it had only scrap value as it was a very small size. The money paid for two gallons of petrol.

Often I used to daydream that I called in at the office and all the maintenance arrears would be there for me to collect. Then I could go on a spending spree and relax for a while from the pressure.

In the difficulties of our life, there were kindnesses. A family we knew had two little girls who were both older than Jacqueline and for several years they sent us parcels of the clothes they had finished with. Jacqueline loved them. The arrival of a parcel was a moment of great excitement with much dressing up and parading in front of the mirror. The great favourite was a silk dressing-gown with fine red and green stripes and a pink hat from Biba.

When I began teaching the invariable element of our weekdays was the nine-to-four routine of the job. The housewife element had to fit into the other hours, as did the gardening, house maintenance, car maintenance and whatever social contact we had. Whatever I may have wished for in terms of a tidy house this was a luxury to me as a single parent. Only a few luxuries were available.

Before too long, we settled down into a working routine. I am not at my best in the mornings so I only did essential chores before work – getting breakfast ready and washing up afterwards, sorting out what Jacqueline needed for a day at school and doing some preparation for the main meal later in the day. Either then or at lunchtime I cleaned the fireplace, getting in coal and logs and took the rubbish to the dustbin. At lunchtime, as well as eating, I tried to organize myself, doing shopping lists or making other plans.

At the end of a day at school we were always ravenous so our first afternoon activity was to get tea and eat! After tea I spent time with Jacqueline. We read stories, played games and took the dog for a walk to the park or across the fields. Sometimes we worked in the garden – something that Jacqueline loved.

Our little cottage had a small garden. The cottage itself was the middle one of a terrace of three. A gate from the street led to these three cottages, as well as two others – one to the left, one to the right. Each cottage had a path from the gate to the front door, dividing the little patch of ground into gardens. Our garden was a triangle, about ten feet wide against the house and perhaps twenty feet long, leading toward the gate. At the apex was a post where the washing-line strung back to the house, tied to a hook high on the wall by the living-room window. At the foot of the post was a beautiful fuchsia bush. Throughout the summer the fuchsia had a splendid array of delicate flowers. I think it was this that inspired us to work on the rest of the patch. We bought seeds at a shop round the corner and planted some annuals, like marigolds and nasturtiums.

After Jacqueline's bedtime, I did the washing-up and whatever cleaning was top of the list. I tended to leave laundering and major housework to weekends, though I usually ended up with jam-making or baking fitting into the evenings.

The kitchen was tiny. It had only one tall cupboard, for food and kitchen things. So everything else had to fit into the cupboard under the stairs. There were boots and shoes on the floor, the small shelves held jams, pickles and other foodstuffs and the remaining space held all sorts of things.

It did not take long to make this house into a home. One of the downstairs walls was made of wood and we had painted it white. Jacqueline fixed all her drawings and paintings to this wall – our own art gallery.

One day Jacqueline asked, 'Why are you always working, Mum? Other people's mums aren't like you.'

'Perhaps other people's mums are not at work all day.'

'Some of them are. Jane's dad cooked the supper when I was there, though. We don't have a dad, do we? I expect that makes a difference.'

I don't think I have ever had the power to earn more money in order to make things easier in practical terms. If we had had a little more money I would not have had to make so many clothes or so many Christmas presents and cards. If I had had more time it might have been possible to find some things at lower prices. But to have more money means to have less time and having less time would have meant even less time spent with Jacqueline at home. My choosing to become a teacher – which had involved a quite gruelling amount of work in my three student years – had resulted in a better payscale, with slightly better hours. I did have more time in the school holidays, which I especially appreciated at times like Christmas when I could make it fun for both of us.

But I did not manage without sacrifice or criticism. What I found was that by its own nature work had to come first.

There were times when I had to go off to work when I would rather have been more available to Jacqueline. For example, the day she first started school I had to take her quite early into her new classroom and leave her with the teacher. There were no other children there and she looked a little woe-begone, trying to be courageous. I rushed out and along the road to my school for the first day. And there were the practical problems. At lunchtime I finished five minutes after Jacqueline and in the afternoon forty-five minutes after. I was really grateful to Miss Gardner, our next-door neighbour, who used to meet Jacqueline from school.

Both Jacqueline and I were extremely hurt that I could not see her in the school play in her first year. As often happens, the performance was in the afternoon, when I was teaching. We had spent a lot of time getting a yellow nightgown turned into the gown of the queen of hearts, sewing red satin hearts all over it. We made a crown out of gold card with red hearts. Jacqueline learned her lines, but said to me very sadly several times, 'I would have liked it if you could come to see me. Lots of mums will be there.'

That stung me. It was one of the times when my frustration reached fury level. When Jacqueline caught flu before the second afternoon performance, she said to me, 'Well, anyway, you haven't missed me in the play today, Mum, have you?'

We did not talk much about it. There were no tantrums – such circumstances were unchangeable.

The house adjoining ours to the south shared the same front porch. Miss Gardner lived there. She was now very old and had lived on a pension a long time. She had been in service and her cottage went with retirement from her job. We met her within a few minutes of first arriving, and Jacqueline quickly made friends, telling Miss Gardner about us. And she told me about Miss Gardner.

It was Miss Gardner who went to see Jacqueline in the school play.

I finished school later than Jacqueline each afternoon, so from her first day Miss Gardner fetched her home. It only involved crossing the road, for the primary school was opposite our house. Every day Jacqueline waited in Miss Gardner's living-room, just like ours, or sometimes she persuaded Miss Gardner to unlock our house so she could fetch some toys.

When Miss Gardner was not too well, we phoned the doctor for her. She was on pills for all sorts of conditions, including her heart, and she told us stories of her palpitations or waking in the night, afraid she would die when no one knew.

Like Jacqueline and me, Miss Gardner liked Marmite – a yeast extract, delicious on toast. One day Jacqueline commented that Miss Gardner only bought tiny jars but we bought a large jar. Why did we get large jars? I explained that I thought you got more Marmite for your money that way. So Jacqueline talked to Miss Gardner, who eventually succumbed to Jacqueline's logic and bought herself a large jar, costing ten shillings (50p) – a vast amount from Miss Gardner's pension of just a few pounds. They were both in Miss Gardner's kitchen when she took it from her shopping basket, fumbled and dropped it on the floor. Both were near to tears. Such a great investment – lost. The pieces were swept up, the stickiness washed away.

It was a sad Jacqueline who met me at the gate with this tale of woe.

'What can we do?' she asked. 'It's too much for Miss Gardner to lose. Besides, she doesn't have any Marmite now.'

Our money always ran out before the end of the month, so did it matter if it ran out a couple of days earlier? Maybe we were better able to survive the loss of ten shillings. We bought Miss Gardner another jar of Marmite.

My impression was that Miss Gardner had not had much to do with children before. She seemed amazed and amused by Jacqueline. If Jacqueline was naughty, she seemed overwhelmed and found it hard to tell me when I got home. Jacqueline herself was either angry or full of remorse. She hated to upset Miss Gardner, so it was more often the latter. They both had difficulty on the day that Jacqueline had come from school and had gone into our house to get a piece of cake from the tin.

Jacqueline had had to climb on a chair to reach the cupboard – it had a glass panel in the door – and when she came to shut the door again she had slammed it rather too hard. The glass had shattered – into the cupboard and onto the floor. To both Jacqueline and Miss Gardner it was a problem of major degree – they hardly knew how to tell me. Miss Gardner was very concerned that I realized it was an accident and that Jacqueline was not being naughty at the time. But I didn't worry too much – from then on we had a cupboard without glass in the door. It was like the day the flap of the kitchen table collapsed and some china fell to the floor. It just meant that we had a teapot with a glued-together lid, and we eventually managed to replace the broken plates.

Jacqueline and Miss Gardner were happy companions. On Saturday mornings Jacqueline would put on an apron to help Miss Gardner polish. When I went on a course to train to teach computers in school, Miss Gardner kept Jacqueline till seven in the evening. They enjoyed having tea together and listening to Miss Gardner's old wireless. But when Jacqueline had a whole day off school and I didn't, I found other friends to care for her. She seemed too full of energy for Miss Gardner to manage for a whole day. When walking, Miss Gardner had to use a stick and couldn't go far. Jacqueline's skipping and bounding would be too much for her.

It is at this point that criticism has been hard to take.

I was always conscious that looking after Jacqueline was one of the most difficult areas of decision-making and already felt guilty enough about aspects that I had not managed to cover effectively. One incident I remember very clearly.

There was a large conference of which I was the administrator. I dealt with booking allocations, fees and general co-ordination. I was also leading workshops. It was hard work. Jacqueline was with Jill, who had helped us many times before and was very capable of looking after her fully.

One of the people on the conference – a mother – stopped me in the hallway. 'I hope you don't mind me saying this to you, but we think you should be spending more time with Jacqueline and less time at working.'

I realized that 'we' meant several of the mothers with whom I was good friends. None of them was a working mother or a single parent. What they couldn't see was that while I had the same *feeling* as them, I did not have the same choices available to me.

I consulted Jill about Jacqueline. 'We're fine,' she said. 'I am enjoying myself, so is Jacqueline. We are off to the beach this afternoon with some other people. Can you come?'

I couldn't, I was working. She continued, 'Jacqueline is looking a bit tired – I think she should have an early night if possible. And you know I would fetch you if necessary.'

I am sure that Jacqueline could have been 'missing' me. But I think not more than usual. For years we had had to learn – both of us – to live with less of each other's time than we would have liked. There were times when she had cried when I had gone to work or to college. She had wanted me around on her first day of school and I had wanted to be there. Neither of us had got what we wanted. It was a cruel feeling that we learned to cope with as the years went by. And we took wholeheartedly all the time we did have together. We became accustomed to the feelings, though they always hurt. No criticism helped – however kindly meant – for me, it just rubbed in the pain of single parenthood.

In general, I gather that single fathers get more sympathy and more encouragement to keep their jobs. Mothers are not expected to keep a job as a priority and these days are expected to live on Social Security in order to be at home for their children. I wonder if this is because the single parent is expected to fulfil only half the roles needed for stable family life – the roles appropriate to their sex.

As a single parent, I have had to find ways to do much more than the woman is expected to do in the traditional family patterns. Many of the 'father' gaps have to be covered – a few cannot be. What are those traditional roles anyway? What do they look like?

Having begun a career in teaching I still found myself with limitations – not just those of skill or ability. Many working mothers do their job to earn a little extra money for the family – they do not necessarily see it as a career. At the same time, many men have a career interest, looking at the long-term prospects and possibilities for promotion, and so on. I seemed to have fallen between the two. I found that the teachers among whom I worked fell into two main groups. Some were looking for promotion and rising through the ranks – these were around after school ended, doing this and that and being quite busy developing their work. Another group was the part-time and married women's group, who rushed away as soon as possible to do their home-making. I was different – I wanted to make my future in teaching, but I was actually only able to be in the second group. It was hard to go back for Parents' Evenings, for school plays, and so on. I would have enjoyed helping with rehearsals and such, but they too were after school.

For a while we experimented in sharing a house with

friends, John and Roz. There was lots of fun and hard work. There were four children altogether as John and Roz had three.

I have shared houses with various other people over the years and talked with lots of others. Sometimes sharing a house works; often it does not. If there is a dominant adult male who believes 'an Englishman's home is his castle', the household is doomed from the beginning. For what is the role or identity of the adults in the second family? What if the head of the second family is a woman? This controlling principle makes her family second-class as far as its status is concerned, and therefore all its members lose their sense of self-esteem and responsibility. I found that sharing a house has to be done on the basis of equal rights for all members.

There have to be some common objectives and respect for differences. Every family has its own little ways, whether in manners or mannerisms, and these can be the irritants when two families share one house.

Sharing with others helped me understand much about family life and being a single parent. There are many aspects of family life that I found were different for a couple – but that doesn't make us less of a family.

There has always been the considerable pressure of general social 'norms' for us to be considered less than a family – the idea that a single-parent family is one that is always looking for a way to become complete, or is worthy of pity because it never can be. The implication of this view is that we do not have the right to be what we are; there is always an undertone that says we should be something else; that we are unacceptable as we are. That Jacqueline and I are a family – one in which I am the only parent – is a statement of fact.

The counterpart, the one I have grown out of, would suggest that I should apologize for our existence and see us as a half-family, an aberration. But parenthood is valid, even if I am the only parent. As the one who has carried responsibility in our family I think I have done it adequately. We have a home, relatives and friends, an identity. We are real and alive, glad to be who we are. All the opinions and judgments that society holds will not change that. If Jacqueline one day marries and has children, I will be a grandparent, just like any other. Our family is a real social entity. We are the Durran family.

6

Mum and Dad Both

One evening I went to a Bible study led by a much-respected old man from one of the free churches. His words were profound and interesting, and as others began to respond and ask questions, I did too.

Then in the nicest possible way he turned to me and said, 'Women should be quiet and submissive. It is an abomination, a sign of the evil of the times that they speak out. They should wait till they get home and ask their husband for such answers. You would do well to learn that!'

I wish I could blot out the experience. I wish it had never been said, but it was.

I was in a dilemma. Marriage was not an option for me then, yet to be labelled and categorized as a person who could speak only through a marriage partner, as half a person, was to condemn us to living death, for Jacqueline and I could not function in a half-existence; nor should we. I was faced with a basic question of personal identity.

I could see that it is difficult for a Christian fellowship to do differently than the rest of society – to live in a different way from society where women are seen as the servants and men the bosses. (Of course, I am speaking of what it was like twenty years ago. But have things *really* changed?) In the church the roles related to being head of a family and its spiritual equivalents were given to men, unfortunately attributed to them as a 'right'. The result was that my status as head of my family was diminished, and as a woman without a husband I was excluded. Such a dilemma had no solution.

This dilemma was an unspoken and undefined factor in our life and friendships and it was only the strength of the friendships that encouraged me to look for an answer beyond the problem. I had to come to terms with being a single parent, as a woman.

I thought about my own childhood, and how I had built up my picture of the world – the world of work and of home, and of parental roles.

At tea-time when I was a child, my father would tell us about his day.

My father ran, with occasional help, a grass-drying plant where huge trailer-loads of fresh-cut grass were brought into the hangar-like shed and tipped onto a conveyor belt. This took the grass into an oven where it was dried out, to make hay. In the same shed was the machinery – hoppers and grinders and mixers – for making cow-cake.

On Saturdays, when my father worked mornings, we children, four of us, often went with him. We saw a different world. There were drivers of delivery lorries and farmers in Land-Rovers. I was a bit afraid of being in the way, yet I loved going to see all the sacks being delivered and collected. The cow-cake smelled of dried grass and molasses. Sometimes when the last sack was being filled from the chute we took the big stick which leaned against the wall and banged the sides of the hopper to make the last bits fall. The sacks were unclipped from the chutes and carried on the sack-barrow over to the storage where the tops were left open so the pellets could cool. We ran our hands through them, and tasted them. Then it was time to close the big doors, fix the locks and climb into the old van that someone had painted yellow with red mudguards. It went with the job – a sort of company car.

Often as tea was finishing, Dad would be reading the day's newspaper. He read out the important or interesting bits of news to us all. In the political world he was a Liberal supporter and we all helped deliver papers and stuff envelopes before elections. He always got a special letter of thanks from some local organizer, which he read out to all of us. From my father's world we learned of business and work, of keeping time and being responsible, of world events and politics.

By contrast, the world of my mother brought news of the village, local events, what was happening to family, friends and acquaintances.

These two different worlds were interpreted to us by my parents. This is a common pattern. It is usual for men to assume that women do not understand the world of business and vice versa. Many mothers I knew when I myself was a mother were very involved in a world that was defined by personal contacts, schools and shops, local development and social life, relatives and family friends. Being an at-home mother or part-time earner of extra cash developed this involvement.

Men, on the other hand, were bothered by the papers, by news items and national concerns. These related to the circles in which men moved.

What about the child of a single female parent? Will she hear of the news and opinions and general conversation that comes from the male circles of concern? As a career woman I found that I did talk about my work-life at home and of what was affecting it. I think I gleaned some of the local events but in fact picked up less of the neighbour-type news. Most of my time was consumed by work and practical housekeeping. There was not much time for chatting to our neighbours or shop assistants or for going to coffee mornings or other social events.

What was our family missing out by having only one parent? In the traditional pattern parenting is not just the sum of male and female roles. One key factor is that because children learn by experience, they model themselves on their parents. Girls learn ways of being a woman from their mothers – of expressing feelings, perspectives on life, patterns of behaviour and responses. Similarly, boys model themselves on their fathers. Jacqueline had a mother who was not the 'norm'. I was involved in work more than being an 'at-home' mother; she had not learned much from the local involvement that I see other mothers bring to their families. When she reached adulthood I wondered if that would make difficulties.

Jacqueline never knew her father. She was far too tiny when she last saw him to remember him. But she had various responses to any idea that I might remarry. She was sometimes quite vehement.

'You wouldn't love me as much, because you would have more people to love. You might have a new baby and then you would love it more than me.'

'What makes you think that?'

'People always love babies the most.'

Finding another husband, a new father for Jacqueline, was not my primary aim in life, to be pursued like my career.

I have recently read reports that suggest it is not necessarily beneficial to remarry, from the child's point of view. It is hard for children to lose a parent and it can be extremely hard to adopt a new one. Children can feel down-graded in the new circumstances. Of course, there are many families in which the single parent has married that do work out well, where the new marriage gives a committed adult relationship at the heart of the family.

Over the years, I had somehow accumulated a little guilt about not having found a new 'father' for Jacqueline – maybe I had no need to feel such guilt.

Indeed, I met very few men who I think could have really loved Jacqueline as their own, whom both of us could have taken fully into our family.

Jacqueline often did for herself things that I think of parents helping a child with, like keeping up with dates and schedules. She used to remind me about things at her school that I might have forgotten. The child of any single mum usually ends up with more responsibility.

One time, Jacqueline wanted to pack her own suitcase for going away. After ensuring that she knew what she was doing and there was a way for me to check or help, I let her. I was glad, for I had plenty to do and this helped me get the work done. I realized later that there would have been a problem if I had given her more responsibility than she could really cope with. In the event, I discovered she also packed a case for her teddy. She had three teddies by now but only one of them had a full set of clothes, including outfits for all weathers and occasions, which the other two were sometimes allowed to borrow.

As a single parent every decision was totally my responsibility and I found it rather heavy sometimes. I could not tell whether I was being over-anxious or just careful. There was no one to ask. What is too risky?

The little side-street where we lived had very little traffic except at the start and finish of the school day when parents' cars passed by, or parked, and great coaches filled the road completely. I remember that in her first term Jacqueline wanted to go to play with Elizabeth who lived about a quarter of a mile away, and she wanted to go by herself. She had to go to the end of our street and cross a busy road, to get to the cul-de-sac where Elizabeth lived.

I took her over the busy road and let her go the rest of the way alone. She had a note in her pocket to give to Elizabeth's mother telling her at what time I would meet Jacqueline to see her back across the road. The plan went well.

I always thought it would have been easier if there had been someone else to talk to. There were days when it all felt too much. I did not notice until I realized I was nagging Jacqueline quite unnecessarily. It is hard not to grumble at the kids on a bad day.

'I am sorry, Jacqueline, I feel tired and in a bad mood. I don't mean to grumble so much.'

'You are grumpy, aren't you? I hope it goes away soon.'

I was gaining a sense of identity from all these experiences, from struggling to be a responsible adult and a single parent. In doing so, I was forced into dealing with many aspects that men more usually had to deal with. Where a family lived was normally determined by the husband's career choices and the choice of house determined by his earning capacity, while a woman's career was normally a back-up and subject to the husband's career. In our life together I found that I was dealing with all these aspects without a partner to be the homemaker. Where the average family might produce a woman who felt and functioned like half a person, I had to function as a whole person – and do the work of two!

7

It's Good to be Alive!

'Mum, I want my dinner now. I'm hungry. Please hurry. Look at this that I wrote today and I did three sums as well. Guess what new words we learned today. My teacher wrote her name down for me to bring home so I could tell you.'

When we both started school Jacqueline and I had our lunches together at home. I rushed out of my class and down the road to where Jacqueline would be watching for me from Miss Gardner's window.

We both wanted to have lunch at home. It was part of the stability of our life – one of the ways we made life work for us in the midst of busy and exciting school days. Most staff stayed at school and chatted in the staffroom, drinking tea and coffee and getting free meals in the dining-room for their duties. I never made my way into the in-crowd, but that was my choice for us. Our lunch was of the instant variety like fish fingers and beans. Then we could both get back to school on time.

At the end of school at four o'clock I sometimes sat down for a cup of tea. That gave me time for a deep breath before beginning again on my other full life. As Jacqueline got older she sometimes came up to my school to meet me, though this was rare as there was such an enormous, daunting crowd of big children to pass, and the coaches drove up and down quite ferociously.

When I got home from school I prepared a leisurely tea and Jacqueline nearly always had a picture to stick on the wall. She knew too that she could have all my attention. She talked and skipped around, telling me about her day.

There was also a walk every day with Edgar – a grey and shaggy Skye terrier, who had become a much-loved part of the family.

Sometimes we walked in the park. Edgar towed us along and Jacqueline tried to walk along the tops of the garden walls as we went. She also ran ahead to see if there were any strange dogs that Edgar might fight with – a sad event always to be avoided. I am sorry to say that despite his size he was a bit aggressive. Once we reached the park he entertained himself while Jacqueline wore out her shorts on the slide.

By the church opposite our house there was a path leading down between the yew trees through a field to a stream. We loved going there. Jacqueline could paddle when she had on her wellington boots and I think it was one of Edgar's favourite places. He was too short to see the rabbits over the long grass, so he was no good at real hunting, but he did have aspirations.

On rainy days or foggy days Edgar got only a short run and we settled down to a game or a puzzle, or some reading. On these sorts of days we made toast by the open fire and pulled the settee up close to the warmth.

Teatime was recollection and reflection for us. It was the only slow-moving time of the day and it was entirely ours to enjoy. Sometimes Jacqueline wanted us to play a game together; other times she played alone or at a friend's house.

Edgar was one more mouth to feed and dog food was expensive. But he was all we had hoped for as a friendly pet. He welcomed us home, took us on walks, barked at strangers and generally made us feel loved.

Edgar could have been more discerning, however. We had a baker who came with a regular order. He had always delivered to Miss Gardner, so now we became customers. Fortunately, she could take delivery of our bread for us while we were out and give it to me when we got home.

The man collected the money on Saturdays. Edgar, however, decided that this unfortunate man was an enemy.

One day Jacqueline was waiting by the door for me to go out with her, with Edgar on his lead. It was a sunny fresh day and the door stood open as the baker came up the path. Maybe Edgar thought he was a threat to Jacqueline because suddenly his hackles rose, he growled ferociously and leapt to attack. Jacqueline hung on to the lead for all she was worth, but Edgar managed to haul her towards the baker, who retreated even more rapidly through the gate and slammed it behind him. Jacqueline fell flat on her face and Edgar ran free.

I paid the baker over the gate, picked up Jacqueline who was yelling furiously at Edgar, and tried to catch the dog – who was so ashamed of his own behaviour that he crawled on his stomach. From them on the baker only came to our house if he was sure the door was firmly shut against Edgar.

On another occasion he worried me a great deal. I woke up at about three in the morning to the sound of Edgar panting and hurrumphing and generally running around. Not sure what the problem was, I let him out of the door to see if the trouble was some essential call of nature. He disappeared for over an hour and I thought we had lost him. While he was away I discovered that he had eaten a whole box of chocolates that we had been given and he had emptied his water bowl. Realizing he must have been very thirsty, I decided to refill the bowl. Eventually he sidled out of the darkness looking very apologetic. His front was wet and I realized he had taken himself to the stream for a drink. When he got home he immediately emptied his water bowl again. He always did have a soft spot for chocolates.

Edgar was a good guard dog, too – as some of my friends found out by experience. There was the time he fastened his teeth round Martin's leg – fortunately Martin was wearing boots and suffered no injury. A burglar would probably have met the same response so, although anti-social, Edgar's behaviour was a little reassuring.

Pet-sitters were not always the easiest to find. There were two goldfish in the bathroom, in an aquarium on the shelf, a budgie and a hamster. I don't think Jacqueline liked any of them as much as Edgar who, being very expressive, appeared quite good at conversation. His ears had different postures to suit his moods, anything from quizzical to sad.

On Saturdays Jacqueline and I enjoyed ourselves. We had no television so we read a lot of books from the library. We had a few records and a radio. So on Saturdays we were off out to the library and to the market in town, where Jacqueline always tried to persuade me to go to the park as it was bigger and better than ours. Sometimes this was the day we went out for tea with friends or visited relatives. There was a good fish-and-chip shop in East Street too, so – even though it was a long way from the bus-stop – we tried to include a visit there.

Our weakness is books – they may be our strength, too! Throughout the years, however short of money we have been, there have always been books. I owned a few, including my college books. While studying I tried to use the library a lot – it was too expensive to buy them.

Once or twice a week when I got home we would jump in the car and go off to the library. Jacqueline always knew what she was interested in – though she often wanted to read half the book while still in the library to make sure it was as good as it looked! Every so often we found such a good book that we could hardly bear to return it. *Hans and Peter* – a story about two boys who turned an old shed into a very pleasant playhouse – was such a favourite that we ordered it from the bookshop so we could have our own copy.

Eventually we discovered a secondhand bookshop. After buying for a while, we would take a box of used paperbacks to sell to the shop and buy some more. Every choice was carefully made.

As our money was limited, we had to be quite careful about how we spent it. I remember the sick feeling I had when I realized how much the Christmas tree lights, which I had just told a shop assistant I would take, would cost. Our clothing money was meagre but a careful budget helped us do many of the things I wanted Jacqueline to enjoy.

As we lived only fifteen miles from Whipsnade Zoo, we went there every six months or so. I wanted Jacqueline to have the chance not only to recognize animals from pictures but also to see and appreciate the real living creatures, their aliveness and character. We used to pack up a picnic and could do the visit very cheaply. The teenagers who enjoyed visiting our house often came along on such trips. I chose to continue to scrape by on the money we spent on housekeeping to give Jacqueline experiences like this. In the same way I could have chosen to finish my work earlier in the evenings if I had not played games with her and gone for walks.

There was a good rail connection with London, so occasionally we went to be tourists. We always took a quick visit to an Art Gallery – a number of small doses are the best introduction. Then we might visit the Tower of London or the Victoria and Albert Museum or the Science Museum – again! We liked Trafalgar Square and Parliament Square and tried to time our visits to hear Big Ben striking.

We also made the best use of our time and limited resources. It is almost a tradition now that we make lots of the presents we give for Christmas or birthdays. A good present does not have to cost a lot of money.

When Jacqueline was very tiny she began to learn to knit and sew. First, she had a piece of cloth and a length of coloured wool and sewed on buttons which she chose herself from the button-box. Only a small step further on was sewing them to Peter Teddy's suit or baby-doll Cleo's dress. Peter Teddy's wardrobe included maroon satin pyjamas and several knitted scarves. All these outfits were kept in a very old suitcase. Before she gave up using it, the collection had grown so big that the clothes had to be squashed down to make them fit in. Every so often there was a dolls' clothes wash day. In went everything, including covers from the doll's pram. Jacqueline swooshed them round vigorously before rinsing them and hanging them on the line. Later she ironed them very carefully, with great care not to touch her fingers with the iron.

In her first term at school Jacqueline was introduced to sewing cross-stitch on Binca canvas and for a while we received lots of purses, table mats and bookmarks made that way. Over the next few years she acquired more skill in embroidery and tapestry. I still have many of the things she made. One that she worked on secretly I still have in my Bible, and it reads, 'Hey y y, cool it mum, its mother's day.'

We had an old blue car which was fairly reliable. Whenever I had a puncture a kind lorry driver stopped and changed the wheel before I could begin to practise the skill my father had taught me. One day the windscreen wipers blew away in the wind as I drove along. But the worst thing that happened was when a double-decker bus drove into me. With the bus towering above me, all I could see was the great gash in its side. I decided the car must be totally squashed and was almost in tears. The car was jammed in the side of the bus and I could see nothing properly till the driver backed it away. The damage to the car was minimal – only the loosening of one chrome strip, which could be rivetted back on in moments! It had been a bit of a shock, however.

Owning a vehicle was the greatest drain on our finances as it consumed so much money in tax, insurance and repairs, apart from its day-to-day running. While I was at college, I had replaced the scooter with a car. Later, we had a minibus which I used to ferry around many of our teenage friends. Our other daily expenses were minimal. We have managed most of our life without a television. When we have had access to one, I have found that we watch perhaps two programmes a week.

While teaching I made contact with many young people. Some were pupils at the school; others were involved in local churches. Over the weeks and months they grew into treating our house like a second home. They came in, ate cakes and biscuits, drank lots of coffee and talked for ever. Some of them became part of our family life – coming with us to London or the zoo, babysitting for Jacqueline or helping round the house. Many of them became fairly involved in the active church life I was in, although most of them – thirty or so – had had no previous contact with any kind of church.

Not far from our village there was a tiny hamlet with a small chapel where the Baptist Church in days gone by had run occasional Sunday services. The minister was happy for the chapel to be reopened and used every Sunday afternoon. Many young people were interested and attended – we usually had a full congregation, as the building only seated about forty. It smelled musty and unused, but having brushed off the dust from the seats we felt quite at home. Jacqueline and I liked to walk there on sunny days.

It was clearly my faith in God that had led me to see the goodness in life itself, both in creation and in humanity. I knew and could prove that by God's intervention there is the possibility of making new what is not good. I was aware of regrettable things and experienced many hard things but I saw that they too were aspects of being alive. I did things wrong. I made mistakes. Life was real – on sad days and on happy days. I came to realize that a fulfilled life is not one which is free of sadness, grief, frustration or other negative feelings. All these are ordinary, predictable human feelings – to try to escape them would be to avoid living. To live long and die of old age is all part of life and God's purpose for people. It is not a regrettable or sad cycle.

I suppose you could say that feelings are human 'colours' in the experience of life. My feelings were mine, and I was responsible for them. There was no obligation on any one else for my feelings – no one need be responsible to make me feel differently or for keeping me happy. I was responsible.

Similarly, no one owed me a living – that was my responsibility. What I did with life was up to me. I saw myself as working within the limitations of my environment, but choosing to tackle those circumstances positively, with 'What shall *I* do now?' rather than saying, 'Someone should do something.'

When I considered the possibility of going to college soon after my first awareness of God, it was the first time I had realized that *I* could do something about the circumstances of my life. It was then that I changed from being passive and subjective, just letting things happen to me, to seeing that I could make decisions about my own life.

So within the flow of experience making up my life I have discovered aspects of my identity and gifts and talents. As I have uncovered my own course through life, I have looked to discover Jacqueline's sense of identity too, for our lives have been inextricably linked together.

Being adventurous, getting out and about, meant that there were always interesting problems to sort out. The early seventies were a time of great activity among young people in the church, with rock and roll making its way in among the more traditional forms of church music. While the secular world saw the first great rock festivals there was a parallel interest within the churches.

There was a phenomenon called 'Festivals for Jesus' – enormous gatherings for young people, mostly in London, where Christian bands and speakers took part.

I took a full minibus of people when we went one evening. Travelling back after midnight, Jacqueline and Edgar both fast asleep, I dropped several of my passengers at their homes. But the rest of us became aware of a knocking sound that seemed to get louder and more pronounced. None of us had any idea what could be wrong. Eventually I pulled into the side of the road and we clambered out. We saw that one of the rear wheels was at a crazy thirty degrees from vertical – a few more yards and it could have fallen off. As it was, the 'bus would go no further.

We were miles from anywhere – we'd left the last village a while ago. Home was too far away to walk. Paddy and Steve thought of walking back the way we had come – they were sure they had seen a phone-box not too long before. Yet who should we phone? No one we knew would still be up at one a.m. We sat on the grass verge pondering the problem. Eventually, a passing policeman gave us a ride home in his patrol car; he probably suspected we would be into trouble if he didn't!

Because of my interest in young people, another teacher invited me to join him in opening and running a youth club in our village. It would be somewhere for the young people to go and we would be paid a wage by the local authorities.

I tried it. The money was helpful and the work was fun. But I did not do it for long as there was too much pressure in being out two evenings a week, having to find baby-sitters, as well as doing more work after a day's teaching. It was too exhausting, so I resigned. Whatever we did in life had to be at least tolerable – as far as I had a choice – and at best enjoyable. Where I had the choice to change stress situations I did. This was one.

I had always had the impression that to go away on a family holiday in the summer was a good thing to do – not that we ever did when I was a child. Jacqueline and I went to summer camps for teenagers two or three times. I went as a leader and as we had little money the fees were waived or reduced. At different times we went to Yorkshire, to North Wales and Sussex. Edgar loved the sea and always turned his nose to the breeze so the wind ruffled his long hair off his face. In North Wales we went up Cader Idris, second highest mountain in Wales, and Jacqueline was very impressed with the railway at Tallylyn and took all her 'Thomas the Tank Engine' books, to check on Sir Handel and the other engines at the station. All the teenage girls at the camps made a fuss of Jacqueline and took her for walks and into the town to go around the shops. So we never did get one of those holidays where a family goes to stay in a bed and breakfast place, or a country cottage, and lazes around the beach with nothing particular in mind. Nearly all the organized holidays for teenagers were full of activity, including a long walk somewhere, preferably up a mountain. Despite her small size, Jacqueline skipped along too, depending on an occasional piggyback when she got too tired.

As teenagers have a different way of looking at life this introduced Jacqueline to a whole new world. When there were workshops Jacqueline often joined in – doing art or tie-dyeing and other crafts.

What made me tackle so many different things, with a job and a home to run as well?

I had a peculiar determination to work hard to enjoy life now, not just in the future. The aims I had were more like milestones than far distant places. I had dreams, but held onto the ones that I believed could be made into reality before too long. Whenever I reached a crossroads – a time or place of choice – I had not necessarily made up my mind beforehand, but I had already decided on the principles that would underlie my choice.

It was more important to me that Jacqueline and I should be happy and fulfilled than that I reach a certain career status or fat bank balance by retiring age. It was good to be alive!

8

Coping – with Help
from our Friends

When you're a single parent, on your own, you need friends. But what sort of friends? And where do you find them? As I grew up, and then went to college, I realized that the over-riding feature of 'a social life' was based on couples, on finding a boyfriend or girlfriend, husband or wife. I felt constantly awkward. I was not able to be involved in the social pursuits of people of my own age-group – but neither could I feel completely happy as a parent, socially involved with people who tended to be much older than me.

Then I made friends with whom I was both a person and a parent. I met the Coppings, Ray and Molly. Their oldest child, Beth, was the same age as Jacqueline and they often invited us over to tea or to spend the day with them. Ray was a teacher and Molly had been – now she was a full-time housewife with three children. Molly and I talked about children and nappies, meals and the practical chores of being a mother. Both of them sympathized with the rigours of my college work and understood about teaching. They took us just as we were.

On the back of their house there was a glass extension where Daniel slept in his pram, and wellington boots were stored, along with big toys like trikes and bikes. Ray's study was, in the daytime, the playroom. As soon as Jacqueline arrived she and Beth and David would rush to the playroom and, seconds later, there was the clatter of the wooden bricks being emptied on the floor. I think they emptied all the toys from the boxes and shelves before they could decide what to play with. On sunny days they headed out to the paddling pool in the garden.

In their generous way, the Coppings made their family life open to us. Jacqueline and I were both completely welcome in their home and we were accepted as a family, without judgment or pressure. Their friendship was a great encouragement to us. There were other families we got to know and with whom we spent time, but probably none as much as the Coppings. Among those people I often felt I was just another parent – but at the same time the differences of being younger than a lot of them and single as well became only a minimal problem.

The Coppings did not live near us so we began looking for a local church to go to on Sundays which had the same warm friendship we had experienced in other places. We met, through a friend of a friend, some people who were wanting to begin a home group for Christians in the area. Over the next year or so we got together a small group, meeting for prayer and Bible study.

Every so often we gathered on a Friday night at the home of one of the group members. Our numbers and our friendship grew. Distances and different work life and church commitments made it hard for us all to keep very closely linked, but we worked at it.

Each time the group met for Bible study Jacqueline came too. At first it was most surprising to experience the freedom to bring Jacqueline to the meetings. Perhaps I ought not to have been surprised, but my impression of Christians at that time was of very dour people studying and praying intently, allowing nothing that might disturb them. Instead I found time and time again that they were very caring people. Their love and concern enabled me to take part in things I would otherwise not even have considered. So, during quiet times of study Jacqueline got out her crayons and books, sometimes interrupting me with a whispered question. Everyone was keen to find her a biscuit and a drink of squash at coffee time. On several occasions she just fell asleep on the floor where she was playing. And so I began to find friends.

On Saturdays, when we had done our bit of shopping, Jacqueline and I often visited Ken, one of these friends. He taught science in another comprehensive school and had a flat near the middle of town. Jacqueline asked me just a few days ago, 'Who was that person we used to visit and roast chestnuts on his gas fire?' That was Ken. In winter, despite the chill outside, we would become quite warm before heading back to the bus-stop and home.

Another couple were Steve and Cynthia who had two children. We visited them a lot. Many times they gave us practical help. For example, when one of the boys from my Maths class was in hospital, Steve and Cynthia lent me their car to take some of his classmates to visit him. And on the morning Jacqueline woke up covered with chicken-pox spots Cynthia looked after her during the day while I was at work. I have no idea what I could have done without that help.

These Christian friends were a great encouragement. We were befriended as a *family* and they invited us to their homes.

Some of the physical work of running a home – fetching loads of logs and coal, or moving dustbins, for example – was rather heavy-going, but I had no choice. Even so, I have had some good neighbours who often offer help – Rick from the farm down the road found his offer to pick up my coal was readily accepted. He really could do the job without feeling he had just died from the effort!

I did not readily ask for help from others after one time when a friend offered to help and I suddenly realized his wife was feeling jealous! That explained why he appeared less and less often. I understood her feeling. Though I had no interest in stealing her husband, she was probably getting a little less of his attention.

Many times I asked myself, 'Whatever can I do now?'

when there was no one to turn to. I found I had more success in staying positive when I refused to conclude that someone else should be helping. I had no husband, committed to the sharing of family life with me, so no one was obliged to help me, frustrated though I was with trying to do the task alone. It was especially those days when I was late and the car would not start. I learned to use jump leads, change wheels, spray Dampstart, check oil and water and petrol, and those kinds of things. I learned to change fuses, wire plugs, look at the tripswitch and switch off the water. Many of our limitations resulting from having no man in the family could be got round somehow.

It was tempting to think sometimes, 'Now if only there were a man around.' But that was more usually related to work requiring some physical strength rather than wanting some man to lean on, or to blame. It was much more fruitful when, without guilt or judgment, I could say to myself, 'Now, something is not going too well here. How can I sort this out?'

While being close to so many other families may have helped, I would not know for years, however, whether Jacqueline has missed out too significantly on experiencing parenthood as a relationship between a man and a woman. Childhood is the most significant time of learning through modelling – taking the 'model' of our parents to guide us in our actions and attitudes. Jacqueline, therefore, has missed out on the model of parenting as a joint task, based on a relationship between two parents.

Jacqueline had seen something of this over the years in the families with whom we had been close – my parents, my sisters, and families such as the Coppings, Hardings and Carvells. Without and before any words, children learn by their experience what life is about. The words they learn in conversation and the books they read may describe, question or modify the picture or concept but the concept itself begins in their experience. A child may learn the facts of life from a book or a film but most of marriage is not sex. It is shared responsibility, decision-making, sharing roles, affection, gifts, ideas, fears and hopes. It is quite different for the single parent to say, 'I have decided...' than for the couple to say, 'Can we talk about what we want to do about...'

Jacqueline had therefore based her concept and understanding of marriage on the marriages of the friends and family we had spent time with.

If as a single mother I had always thought, 'I must be married before I can cope with this family,' then I could have had little hope of good friendships. I would have been always trying to snare every eligible man into my problems – and some ineligible ones too!

One aspect of growing up in a society, and being in a church, that defines a family as being under the 'headship' of a man, is to be indoctrinated into believing that every woman needs to be under the protection of a man and can only find her identity in society through him.

Whatever I was raised to believe, I have discovered that life goes on without there being a man to perform these roles. I looked after our rights and learned to deal with the ins and outs of the system. I dealt with tax forms. And if we were physically in danger, I did what any other citizen does – man or woman – I phoned the police. I suppose women are potentially more vulnerable to violence, less able to defend themselves but many women do live alone and are fine. I got used to taking reasonable security precautions.

Of course I was sometimes afraid, but my many experiences of being safe lead me to believe that mostly we *are* safe. Indeed I had married friends who were far more afraid than I was, because they never have got used to being in a house alone. I found my worst fears are inside me, in my imagination, more than anything real on the outside.

The lack of status or identity was harder to come to terms with or avoid. Socially it is hard for the single parent to find a place. A woman going alone to a pub or restaurant was a bit of a misfit, and her purpose in being there could be totally misinterpreted! Who would I go with? It is not always easy to find a single male friend who will oblige on the basis of friendship alone.

One friend, Bill, teased me several times for being a 'women's libber'. I denied this as I did not see myself as having set out to get equal rights for women. But I do now see that many of the issues I have tried to come to terms with as a parent have resulted in my saying that single parents, and women who are single parents, must not be treated as second-class parents. I differ very considerably, probably, from many in the women's lib movement in that I am, in the absence of a marriage, happy to be celibate. Sometimes there is pressure against that for we live in an environment that keeps telling us through advertising and the media that sex makes the world go round.

Fortunately, the stigma of social disapproval of the single parent has gradually decreased. When people realized I was a single parent they grew less embarrassed and less disapproving, more interested. Because a moral question was part of my heritage – that the concept of a single parent was somehow wrong by definition – I have had guilt of my own to deal with, as well as feeling the judgment of others. My marriage was a bleak and miserable failure from the start. I don't think I did any better in the circumstances than my husband – I had no idea how to make ours a good relationship, so I could not do a whitewash job. So I was in the early days very susceptible to the 'tut-tut's' from others. As I forgave myself, and us, and the circumstances, I was able to free us to be the people we have now become.

We were succeeding in our family life, in all its practical aspects. Despite the major effort of getting established, we were mostly reasonably organized and balanced. Sometimes I looked around for adults to share my life with, and not just my life but the lives of the teenagers who had made our house their second home. Was this a sense of unease I was beginning to feel?

I enjoyed teaching once I got settled into it, and the Christian fellowship was the scene of lots of fun and work. It may have been that these good things, despite being good, somehow worked against each other. I did not think that I had reconciled them and, despite some signs to the contrary, I began to feel I was perhaps doing them badly, while enthusiastically.

When she started school, Jacqueline had been the only child in her class without a father. Then gradually there were others. But most of the social structures were designed to help the two-parent family and the at-home mothers. I wondered whether Jacqueline would experience negative responses among her peers.

One of Jacqueline's friends, Mark, had played with her lots of times, when they were both about five. One day they were playing mothers and fathers and he gave her a funny look, and I heard him say, 'Oh, you don't have a daddy, do you.' Because of his relationship with his own mum and dad I think Mark felt sad for Jacqueline and obviously puzzled that this particular form of role-play was a game in which she was very poor at keeping to the rules.

Over the years, society has accepted higher divorce rates and changing family structures. It has become normal for a high proportion of children to spend some of their growing years with only one parent – the experience of up to one–eighth of families in the middle of the eighties.

Once I was standing in for a teacher who was absent at school. Dave was developing a new course on relationships, and he had asked the children to think of their own family relationships and then draw a family tree. I drew an example on the blackboard. Lots of the children responded.

'Please, miss, my dad has married another lady and my mum has married another man and I live with my granny and grandad. How shall I draw it?'

'I live with my auntie, and I don't know my mum's name.'

'Do my mum's children all have to be written in and my new dad's children as well? It makes quite a lot!'

These children were not worried about any social stigma, but were more concerned with how to describe and live with their circumstances.

When I worked with children in Sunday School or workshops, I was always very careful on this particular topic. I did not assume that every letter should be addressed, 'Dear Mum and Dad . . .' and made sure that illustrations of families are not drawn simply as mum, dad, a girl and a boy. I wanted no person and no family to feel defined as a failure or unacceptable.

Before I wrote all this down someone sent me a letter. It said, 'Read Mary Craig's "Blessings".' I did. She describes the painful traumas of life with clarity and compassion. And out of the ashes come people with a compassionate heart and a spirit to serve others. Who would choose to repeat the hard soul-destroying experiences of life in order to learn compassion? Yet it is in the hard times that good things may emerge from the ashes.

Several times I had faced what seemed to be insuperable barriers and I had gone down in a silent inner spiral into the darkness of despair, where all kinds of strange impressions overwhelmed me. I learned in those times to wait for the peace at the heart of the storm and slowly to allow myself to grow up from that new place.

In one way, the worst time was the year following

Jacqueline's birth. All my life since then had been spent crawling out of that awful hole. I had discovered that I did want to live and that I enjoyed living. Despite all the depressing things that happen in the world, I was glad to be alive and I had hope – hope that was not just for myself but for others who seem to be struggling to survive, like flowers that push their way up through the concrete path and between the paving stones. I could believe that it was possible because I had struggled up through my own cement path – not with bitterness and retaliation, but to some measure of compassion. My attitude to what had happened had no pity in it and I wanted it never to be in my relationships to others.

Also during this time I experienced accepting friendship – not people taking over from me, leaving me a helpless vegetable, but people who helped me find the space to grow. I had found time to grieve, not for a physical death but for all the other deaths that have been part of my death to life experience. At the time I had been unable to carry any more than the day's own pain and hold myself firm against feeling it too deeply. It became a shell against vulnerability.

Looking back, maybe I have always been a little afraid that what I received would not be good. One of my earliest memories is about Christmas. On Christmas Eve, I went with a friend's family to visit her relatives who all gave her presents. At home the following morning – Christmas Day – I woke in my cot, to hear the rest of my family making a noise downstairs with shouts and laughter. I crept blearily down to join them, and sat watching my brother and sisters unwrapping all sorts of things from their stockings. My sister turned to me, 'Where's your stocking?'

'I haven't got one,' I answered.

My sister who was a year older than me was a lot more knowing. 'Yes, you have. We all have. It's by your bed

71

upstairs, I'll go and fetch it.'

I did not expect the treats to be for me. So I hung back from the centre of things so as not to be noticed.

Another time I remember bursting into tears under my bedcovers, thinking that my dad, who always kissed us goodnight, had missed me out. He heard me and came back to give me another kiss.

As a child I loved to be around him to watch him working, just as Jacqueline did years later. Though I hardly realized it at the time, his acceptance of and care for Jacqueline and me, though never spoken of, helped us immensely. He never challenged, accused or demanded repayment. It was not till after his death that I recognized his compassion that enabled Jacqueline to have such an enjoyable early life when I was least able to cope with all she needed as a child. He never spoke of the pain I was feeling but was not insensitive to it. His own childhood had been hard as his parents had broken up and gone separate ways leaving him with an aunt.

Among these people and so many more I had begun to take hold of the fragile hope that life was worthwhile. This was not a rosy life-will-turn-out-right-in-the-end viewpoint, rather a recognition that life would always have ups and downs and that downs are to be lived through, but are better with a little help from friends.

I was, however, carefully guarding all the ground I was achieving. I was untrusting and not disappointed when I was let down – it was only what I expected. I was strangely unhurt by a number of external pressures. For example, the snubs I received from fellow teachers when I gave up teaching for a new life were a little bewildering, yet they were deflected by the kind of faith I had in those days. I had a strong personal faith which rode over many difficulties and I was determined to do what God called me to do.

The strength of my will to live had made me find a way

of building a thick shell around myself, which was less and less penetrated by the pressures of ordinary life. And, despite the apparent strength of my faith in God, that too was at that time part of the shell.

9

Breaking the Shell

A week after Jacqueline's eighth birthday we moved to join the Community of Celebration. It was another new beginning.

Our arrival was announced by Edgar who leapt out of the minibus, with much growling and woofing, to attack Ben, a rather friendly mongrel who did not want to be anyone's enemy. Being small, Edgar's policy was based on attack being the best form of defence. Dogs belonging to Christians are not any more Christian than anyone else's dogs!

On our first evening in this new home, still bewildered with its newness, Jacqueline and I went to evening worship where all the community members, including the babies, met for a short time together. People were seated in a circle of chairs and some sat on the carpet in the middle. Jacqueline sat very close to me, peering at these new faces. Until that time we had met only the travelling group – the Fisherfolk. Here were many others. We sang and prayed together. It was only a day or two later that I looked round for Jacqueline at worship time to find that she was already sitting with Tim, a newly-found friend.

Over the months leading up to that moment I had not realized how much I had wanted to see a kind of family home that was strong enough and easy-going enough for the many people, including teenagers, I met – a place where all sorts of people could be friends together. When I arrived home at the end of a hectic day, who was going to laugh and cry with me? Occasionally there was someone; most often there was not. I had tried to convince myself I was just lonely and must learn to adjust to it.

All these thoughts and feelings had run together till I knew I was looking for something more in life. I was looking for a family life where not only single parents but also others – single and lonely and young – could belong. I was beginning to see that life *could* work for a single parent – but what of all those other people who were looking for a family to belong to and a home to live in?

I began to look to the church for this way of life – realizing that New Testament life described the qualities I was looking for. I knew what I wanted, yet it was hard to describe in words what I had never seen. So I was restless, wondering.

It was then that I had been invited to work on a Christian conference which a group called the Fisherfolk were leading. These people led worship services using both traditional and contemporary forms. The music was both simple and inspiring. The teaching workshops helped people to use the arts – music, drama, dance and art – to develop their own skills for leading worship in local churches. There were single and married adults, some with children, working together as a family. All of them belonged together. They were a family of close friends and in them I recognized what I had been searching for; I received an enormous boost to my sense of hope.

We got on very well together and to my surprise they invited me to help lead the conference workshops with them. I got to know Jodi and Jon very well as we worked on drama together. By the end of the week I knew I wanted us to be part of their Community family, and they invited us. I accepted, knowing this would mean moving house and job again, for another beginning.

The Fisherfolk themselves were the travelling team from a group of people that the Bishop of Coventry had invited to his diocese. Many churches around the country then invited the team to visit and share an exciting experience of praise and worship in their own local churches. The

Community of Celebration, home of the Fisherfolk, had grown up in the Coventry diocese, and our move to join them coincided with their move to Reading in Berkshire. The Bishop of Oxford recognized the group as a community within the Anglican church and we were members of the local parish church, in many ways just like other church members.

At home within the community there were households – groups including one or more families and single people, each living as a family, working out life together. Daily work, daily chores and the general ordering of life was the responsibility of the adults in the household. Some people had jobs locally in Reading and the nearby area, others of us ran the house and cared for the children. Two or three worked full-time to prepare a new hymnbook for publication while a number of us were travelling quite frequently at the invitation of churches around the world. It was patterned like traditional religious communities; though unlike monks and nuns there was no uniform here, nor indeed the traditional vows.

Jacqueline and I formed a household with Virginia, another single parent, and her four children, and several single people. As a community we ran a family business which provided the majority of our income. Virginia, a social worker, was one of several people who worked outside the community. Together we sorted out how to spend our money, how to spend our leisure time, how to care about our common concerns and how to help one another. It was essentially family life on a larger scale.

Jacqueline at eight was very skinny and blonde-haired. She was often thoughtful and quiet. Some of her pensiveness had arisen from sensing that I was anxious about our family concerns when the two of us lived alone. Living in this new, larger family she relaxed a lot. We felt at home in a way we had never felt before.

Jacqueline quickly made friends with others her own age

and in these friendships her sense of fun came out. She was naughtier, which, I think, was because she was less anxious and more secure, and had more opportunity. Anyway, I had to keep a closer eye on her.

Alison was nine and came with her family from Beaconsfield. She and Jacqueline were ingenious at working out how to get what they wanted. One afternoon after school they set up a stall with a variety of their old toys on it, selling them to the other children for a few pence each. They were sure they needed the money. At school Jacqueline was moved ahead a year, so she worked with Alison and Martha, another good friend, with whom she spent a great deal of time.

Jody was younger than Jacqueline and an outdoor type – most unlike Jacqueline in that sense. They made mischief together. One day they were playing on the roof, three floors up, having found the way out of an upstairs window. Another time they, with several others, crawled through a tiny trapdoor into the gap between the cellar ceiling and the floor of the ground level rooms, in amongst the heating pipes and wires. We lost them for the whole afternoon while all the time they were under the floor listening to us searching!

There were six girls, with Naomi and Tricia as well, at that wonderful age when everything in life is giggled about. One Saturday evening party around the turn of the year, we awarded all sorts of funny prizes to people. To the six girls we gave an award for being the Giggliest Gaggle of Girls.

One of my first new friends was Virginia. Her youngest son, Carl, was Jacqueline's age. When the children got together and presented a play from the Winnie-the-Pooh stories, Carl was Pooh Bear. Quin, Virginia's eldest son, was a teenager who was always interested in the world around. Jacqueline asked him endless questions about the world and politics and pop music. Quin was in a band with a few of his school friends. Quin and Jacqueline used to watch Monty Python together.

One evening the monks from Nashdom Abbey came to a buffet supper with the Community. There must have been about a hundred people. Suddenly I became aware of Jacqueline sitting on a window-seat absolutely shaking with laughter. There was no one near, her plate was lodged beside her. I went over and sat next to her.

'What's happened that's so funny?' I couldn't see anything that warranted the response.

She exploded into more giggles. The more I asked, the more she laughed, the joke grabbing her every time she tried to speak. I gave up and found out much later that she'd suddenly remembered a scene from Monty Python.

What made this new home different and special for us?

I got very frustrated when people suggested or implied that the single-parent family was an inadequate environment for children to grow up in. I was angry not because they were wrong but because ivory-tower social analysis is not the same as caring enough to help make life different! So the learned words smacked of patronising attitudes and growing clever at the expense of those they study. It was true that statistics about single parents were depressing. And it was an enormous relief to be among people who knew that single parents have not got it all made, and who want to work out life together so that it is better for everyone.

The change in my own attitudes did not happen overnight. For instance, one day Ray discovered that I had just carried two very heavy suitcases down from the second floor and across to the car park. 'Why didn't you ask me to do it?' he asked.

I was so used to being the only one to do such work, it had never occurred to me to ask.

Here in this new large family we lived and worked in a web of interdependence. It was a shock after my previous way of life. I felt as if I was in a foreign land, with a different language and a different culture.

It was strange to find Virginia enjoying Jacqueline's company as if she were one of her own children, and making her clothes along with the others. I found it hard to believe that this was not a criticism of how I had managed so far, but it was not.

Through my friendship with Virginia I was encouraged as a parent. She wanted to know about Jacqueline and how I was raising her, why I did what, and she listened carefully to my responses.

'How have you made Jacqueline so responsible and well behaved?' she asked.

I had not really thought about *how* I was doing it till then. Through all our chatting together I began to understand our family life a lot more.

The development of these family relationships in the community had their ups and downs. I had an enormous row with John about Jacqueline.

'She is great. She is mature and responsible, I agree,' he said. 'But emotionally she looks only to you, and lets no one in. I don't want her to grow up that way or she will never really feel loved by anyone else.'

My first response was to be very angry with John or anyone who got involved with our relationship. But after several days of simmering down I realized the truth of what was being said. I needed to be open before Jacqueline could receive love from other adults, especially men. In our new family, she grew to feel loved by John, sometimes sitting on his knee, something she had only ever done with my father.

I saw how being the child of a single parent had limited her, but I could only admit it as a new way opened up, and I saw that John's love and sense of responsibility for children was not limited to his own and Margo's children.

Such openness can only happen where there is trust, and trust is a fruit which grows gradually. It took me a long time – more than a year – before I could feel really open, even with these people who were totally trustworthy. Society and my experience of life had taught me to defend myself. As a young person I had believed that the one place that was free from betrayal was marriage. It had proved to be a romantic and false notion. I was guarded now against everyone. Gentle, continued exposure to this new experience of friendship was needed to build the steps towards total trust and to remove my defences. I saw that I was also guarding Jacqueline against trusting people, against being emotionally open, for that could result in hurt. For up to that point in my life openness had resulted in such despair and such a sense of failure that I wanted neither of us to experience it ever again. So I was internally programmed against open, trusting relationships. I only learned to be open again by a slow step-by-step building process that was excruciatingly painful because of my previous experience. John was the first person directly to challenge my right to withdraw into a shell – a shell that kept out all love relationships.

In the community I worked in an office – reception and general administration. Its windows looked out onto lawns and gardens, a field and woodland. One day I stood gazing out, hardly seeing the beauty of the view, for I knew I had the choice of whether to break out of my shell, or not. I knew that if I chose that openness in friendships I would never be able to back out without being very hurt, again. But I also knew that if I did not choose to go beyond my shell, I would never feel loved, nor would Jacqueline. So I chose the risky course of breaking out of the shell, fighting against the strong defensive feelings that welled up.

Becoming interdependent was like being joined together as threads in a web. We were becoming one family together – Virginia's, John and Margo's, other parents and single people – and my concern became not only for *my* child and *my* family but for *our* children and *our* family. It was, though unwritten, an adoption into one family.

As a working parent, I was very involved with what went on outside the home. Running a home and family things came after that, fitting into the gaps. Sylvia was mostly an at-home mother and had been a friend of ours almost from the moment we met. Jon, her husband, was a member of the Fisherfolk team and was away from home quite frequently. In the first few weeks after we arrived their second son, Justin, was born. With Sylvia, Jacqueline enjoyed many home-based activities. She helped with the baby, took him for walks and played with him. She would visit Sylvia and talk to her about children and family life. Through being with Sylvia, Jacqueline learned much about being in a larger family with two parents and more than one child.

'Jacqueline, will you help me clean the big fridge on Saturday?' When the chores needed to be done, Jacqueline liked most to help Sylvia.

'Sylvia says you do it like this,' she would explain to me afterwards.

In our life together before we lived in community I had not thought out fully how Jacqueline could learn to do the routine jobs of housework, cleaning and cooking and childcare. Many times I had done my chores after she had gone to bed, so there had been no time for her to learn them from being with me. She learned so much from Sylvia. Often Jacqueline helped her cook and eventually she copied all Sylvia's recipes into a card index box of her own.

All the children, once they were seven, joined a washing-up team. This was a major chore, doing the dishes for seventy or more people. On Saturdays, and in school holidays, children helped with our work. On Saturdays they helped in the afternoon, and on holidays for part of

81

the morning. For instance, Jacqueline worked with Jon at cleaning the long hallway. There was hoovering to do, corners and shelves to dust, furniture to polish. It wasn't arduous, though Jacqueline grumbled sometimes. She and Jon had long conversations as they worked.

The Community had a five-line telephone system. A small exchange near the front door switched calls through to various offices and households. We taught Jacqueline and others her age how to operate the system and this became a favourite Saturday chore for them, two at a time. It was not very busy in the afternoon, so we were fairly sure they would not be overwhelmed with numbers of calls.

The needs and concerns of each family became the needs and concerns of all of us. Grandparents have a special place of affection in a family's life, and are very important to the children. John and Sylvia's parents all lived in the United States, so whenever Jacqueline and I visited my parents, Michael and Justin wanted to come too. We nearly always went together and my parents enjoyed being 'adopted' by the boys.

'We're going to Granny's on Sunday,' Justin would tell everyone.

Two years later, when Michael started school, Jacqueline was like a big sister, helping him find his way and showing him what to do.

Until this time our family life had had a protective shell around it. A good shell, with few gaps. We could make it financially and socially at a level that was tolerable. But I had felt frustration and despair resulting from the competing demands and pressures of three equally significant aspects of my life. These – work-life, home- and family-life and church-life – had been completely separate and seemed to be at war with each other. All of them were good and they were what I wanted to be doing, but I had not reconciled the lack of integration between them. In the Community of Celebration family all these aspects of life were integrated and managed together. Our business and our family life and our worship were integrated and helpful to one another.

It was during this year I was able for the first time to go with other parents to Jacqueline's school on Sports Day and for the Christmas Concert. I felt like a real mum.

The Community virtually ground to a halt on the day of the school Christmas concert. Between us, we had lots of children at school and all the parents, mums and dads, arranged for time off work to go down to the school. There were not many other dads there from the village – probably because they couldn't get time off. Even so, we had not calculated how early parents would arrive for a two-thirty start. We crowded in along the back row of the hall and watched all the events.

Jacqueline's class presented a play in which she took part and, along with various other classes, sang old and new Christmas carols. The play was unspectacular but it was great to be there.

At Parents' Evening, I got a shock too. I wondered why Jacqueline's teacher looked so familiar – she reminded me of someone – then I realized she had been at my college. She, equally puzzled, couldn't work out who I was. While my face was familiar, the name did not fit the person she remembered. I had changed back to my maiden name after college. She enjoyed having Jacqueline in her class and I was encouraged to find her working with the kind of teaching principles I had considered important from my training. One evening she came with her husband to visit us at home and stayed for supper.

The next summer the Sports Day was bright and sunny. Parents gathered all over the playing field and were gently marshalled out of the way by eager children. Ice-creams were on sale and Jacqueline was a determined participant in the sack race, as well as running. She and her partner, Martha, laughed so hard in the three-legged race that they simply sat down in the middle of the course and could go no further.

This new family was based on our choosing together to look after the lives and concerns of all of us, in trust and love for one another. As a single parent for whom marriage had ended in trauma, this was a new start on love and trust in relationships. Looking at it another way, I now had three choices for my life, where only one had existed previously.

Up to this time I had followed one choice – the only one I had had – that of finding a way to cope alone. Given that there are hard days and times of depression, this had been a workable alternative for me. It had the advantage of giving me the choice of career development, and a place to live. More, my married friends say, than they have, as their choices are limited by working this out with their partners. My shell protected this way of life very effectively.

In theory I could have had another choice – to remarry. But my defensive shell meant this was virtually impossible. If I had taken that step, the marriage would have broken up because of my defences. The renewal of my ability to live in trust and openness with others was the beginning of a new possibility that we could again become a two-adult family!

A third choice was also apparent. There was the possibility of living a common family life with others, as a single-parent family in the midst of a bigger family. Jacqueline and I would not be an isolated family working out our life alone. Jacqueline and I were not the 'poor' ones being helped by everyone else. We, as did all the others, both gave and received, in interdependence.

My faith in God had for years been the focus of my life. This did not change, but my perspectives did. The struggle to survive through Jacqueline's early years had made me totally dependent on God, as a child is dependent on a parent. Children grow up and, having learned from parents, begin to take responsibility for what happens. When only the tiniest setback threw me into despair, I found that God helped me over some major hurdles, through the care and help of other people. But there is a next stage in growing up. The good parent does not prevent setbacks and the child learns to pick herself up when she falls. So God has not stopped me having normal human problems and pain and I have learned to deal with them more positively.

I grew beyond a need to think of God as a kind of fairy-godfather. When we run into normal human problems, the love we experience from friends makes a lot of difference. I had to face the hard fact that because we are human, we Christians are not protected by God from normal human problems – except in some exceptional circumstances, occasionally.

When I saw how much other people could and would love Jacqueline and other children I began to see another new perspective. God really does love all children.

I became aware that to be a Christian is to see the order with which God has made the whole of creation and, by growing into a full experience of that, to become more fully human. Being among friends meant that we had continuing encouragement. God gave us an 'ordinary' human life which included suffering, difficulty and problems. In the early days of my faith when I was so dominated by fear my prayers were mostly requests and pleas. But coming to terms with my fear of travelling, of accidents, of unforeseen horrors, happened in the growth process. Now prayers were more listening than asking.

My Christian faith and experience required me to be still enough in myself to hear God through the circumstances of life as well as through the words of the Bible.

The friendship of the Christians among whom Jacqueline and I now lived set me free both to love and to cry. As we are free to laugh and cry, to live with our joy and our pain, we can have compassion for others. This freedom also helped me give up my bitterness, guilt and my tendency to judge.

My faith in God had reinforced the shell, so I had coped enough to manage life as a single parent. But this new experience of friendship broke that original shell, allowing me room to be an adult and a parent in a larger family. My understanding of God was now greater – he is the deliverer of the needy and desperate and the caring Creator, working for harmony in all he has created.

When Jodi and I wrote a song together the chorus was based on a verse from Paul's letter to the Romans, chapter eight, using the J. B. Phillips version: 'And all creation's straining on tiptoe just to see the sons of God come into their own.' The children of the community joined together and made a dance to go with the song. We were all coming into our own.

10

We Laughed and Cried

In our new family we laughed a lot. I had not laughed so much since I was a child. I was used to more sober gatherings or else laughing at the antics of the professional comedians on film or television. But this was a large family full of fun and laughter.

After supper on Saturdays we gathered from our various homes for what we called a celebration. Sometimes it was a birthday party and always it was an event that included everyone. Towards the end of Saturday afternoon, Margo, Martha and I would sit in our office and come up with ideas for the evening's entertainment.

There were many children in addition to Jacqueline and her group of friends. Martha, one of the single adults, got them to do little plays based on the stories of Winnie-the-Pooh. She had discovered that, with a narrator adding an occasional sentence, many of A. A. Milne's original stories could be turned into plays. Martha produced the scripts and gathered all the children for a couple of hours rehearsal ready for the evening performance. Anna, who was very sensible, was Owl. Jody was very bouncy and energetic so she became Tigger. Jacqueline was always Rabbit. The little children, who were not yet able to read or even rehearse well but wanted to join in, all came as Rabbit's friends and relations. When Winnie-the-Pooh discovered the North Pole, Rabbit's friends and relations had gone as well, so Martha found a good way to include as many of the children as possible.

A few months later I was given a book of plays based on the stories of Paddington Bear. The first of the plays was his arrival on Paddington Station. Jacqueline played Paddington. She was rather good at this. She was able to keep very serious whatever problem arose and, rather like the real Paddington, she seemed oblivious of the chaos she caused. There was a wonderful scene where Paddington was with Mr Brown – Phil – buying a very large creamy foam 'cake' on the station. They bought one each from Gary, who had a refreshment trolley laden with drinks and foamy cakes. Paddington wanted a drink as well as a cake, so she placed her cake on the floor beside her while she picked up a cup. Just then she stepped and skidded in the cake and sat right on it, sending foam everywhere. As she struggled to rise, Gary tried to help, reaching across the trolley, and knocked a dozen cups of water all over her. She spluttered and jumped, getting her head under Mr Brown's plate – he was leaning over to help, too – and his cake landed all over his face. It was our first very effective attempt at slapstick – an excellent custard-pie routine!

All our children had one particular habit in common. As they rushed in from school, their minds set on getting a snack and a drink, school bags and coats and bits and pieces were immediately strewn everywhere. For the adults there was a constant need to remind them by saying, 'Please hang up your coat first.' One Saturday we adults made a sketch of what this looked like, with adults playing the parts of the children. It was extremely entertaining – though I do not remember a significant change in the general arriving-home chaos.

One year everyone wanted to have a New Year party, but because we wanted to include all the children as well, we had to be ingenious. That evening we moved all the clock hands forward so that we were three hours ahead of the rest of the country. We saw the New Year in together at an hour that was more accurately nine in the evening. The younger children were overjoyed at being able to stay up so late!

On several occasions we gave each household a subject or title and gave them thirty minutes each to produce a play! Then we all watched several plays, each only five minutes long. Our creativity was stretched and grown. For many of us this was a totally new experience – acting, playing, celebrating – with the sole purpose of enjoying ourselves together.

Spring Bank Holiday came. Should we work as usual or have a day off and how might we use a day off? We decided to hold our own 'carnival'. There were stalls and games and races. Everyone came in fancy-dress costumes, as characters out of history or fairy tales or fantasy. I saw Alice in Wonderland and the Mad Hatter. Jacqueline was Tweedledum or Tweedledee – it was hard to tell which. Out on the lawn were games, such as guessing-the-number-of-beans-in-the-jar. Who could guess the weight of the cake? There was a clown with a very large bunch of balloons which he eventually gave away, to the children mostly. Sylvia and Carol set up a barbecue and served hot dogs for everyone.

Our sports included balloon races, where contestants ran a distance with the balloon then had to sit on it to burst it, and a bun race, where sticky buns were hung by strings and contestants had to eat one without using their hands. Then there was a pie-eating contest. Four teenage boys, one young father and a teenage girl joined in. The girl won after getting to her sixth twelve-inch-wide, thick-pastry pie. The teenage boys entered a cycle race that included riding across a six-inch wide wooden 'bridge' across a local pond. None of them fell in.

When this large family gathered together it was hard to find appropriate responsibility for the children to carry. Making a successful barbecue for ninety people is a skilled job and the children could not organize this. So we formed a Children's Club where the children themselves could build a fire and cook outside and tackle other projects together. They camped and had outings. Their favourite was to toast marshmallows over an open fire and eat them squashed between two chocolate biscuits.

In the summer Bob and I took the whole of Jacqueline's age-group to Wales in a minibus and a camper-van. The girls would sleep in a tent; the boys in the van. There were thirteen children aged seven to eleven. We arrived at a beautiful camp site, near Dolgellau, and pitched our tent in a good open space twenty yards from the river and far enough from the toilets that visitors to them would not disturb us.

Then the rain started. It poured in absolute torrents. We cooked in the van and tried to pass plates of hot supper into the tent without them filling with rain. We slept all night huddled into the middle of the tent, away from the wet walls. It didn't stop raining till mid-afternoon when all the children seemed to have been soaked through several times and we had heaps of dripping clothes to dry in the local launderette, as well as one or two sleeping-bags. When Martha fell in the river in her last dry clothes and no one had any more to lend her, we called it quits and packed up to go home. We finally got thirteen sleepy, dirty children home at around midnight. There were a few photos of a shivering cold bunch of children huddled on a rock near the foot of Snowdon – we had driven past it on the way home so we could say we had been there. The top was overcast in a mist of drizzle and cloud.

Jacqueline and I had only occasionally experienced being part of this kind of celebration before and that was not in an environment where everyone – adults *and* children – had fun together. There had been a few social events for adults and parties for children. Almost always the events and gatherings had had a dual purpose – there was some functional reason, such as raising money towards a good cause or common need, as well as having fun. Apart from my own family at home, I do not think I had ever met people who got together for fun and no other reason! To enjoy ourselves and simply to enjoy being together reminded me of Latin-American carnivals, when everyone abandons the pressures of ordinary life to have a festive time together.

To talk of celebrating with times of laughter could be escapism. But we found we had to come to terms with grief and sorrow, too. Could we celebrate the whole of life with its joys and sorrows? We were not immune to sadness and grief; instead we had to find a realistic way of dealing with the sorts of things all human beings have to deal with. Being Christians does not separate us from tragedy, nor should it, for that would be to imagine we can become something other than human.

It is a little dangerous to laugh so heartily because you get used to having feelings and expressing them with great abandon. So when you are sad you may cry as heartily as you laughed. I did not realize this consequence at first. For the whole of my life my feelings had been firmly held in check, under cover. Suddenly I found myself expressing pain as readily as laughter. Just as surprising was the easy way this family of Christians were comfortable with such feelings and expressions. They neither tried to change them, nor were they embarrassed to be a shoulder to cry on.

I remember once that the children had their own particular sorrow. Jacqueline and her friends found some baby birds in the garden. For a whole weekend the children went every couple of hours and fed the babies using an eye-dropper to give them milk. Miraculously they survived till Monday evening. But when the children came home from school the birds were dead. We had a troop of sad and tearful eight- and nine-year-olds. They eventually decided to have a funeral. Having discovered a suitable cardboard-box coffin and dug a hole in an unused part of the vegetable garden, they invited us to the service. We followed some handwritten service sheets and sang from hymn-books the children had brought for us. We all shared their sadness. But there were greater sorrows.

One married couple had joined us, with their two children. The wife was very ill with leukaemia and had been for a number of years. It would have been exciting if she had been miraculously healed – that does happen to people sometimes. However, this woman died within a few months and we were the friends that were to support their smaller family through the time of pain and stress.

Less than a year later there was a cot-death. A baby boy, who had been born ill but then appeared to be thriving, died for no apparent reason, just a few months old.

How could we be reconciled to life when these people died without living to old age and a full life? We could not have survived in our faith, open as we were, unless we could be reconciled to suffering. We accepted our grief, not allowing the enormity of it to force us to despair, but letting it help us come to terms with life.

As long as we were determined to love one another, to laugh together and to care for one another, then we would cry too. A Paul Simon song says, 'If I never loved I never would have cried...a rock can feel no pain and an island never cries.' It seems to be one of the myths of modern romanticism that there can be a pain-free state in which loving and being loved can exist without tears and pain. It is a popular aspiration of recent generations. To support it we contrive ways of living in protected isolation, because we want to avoid being hurt. But all of us want to feel loved. Hence the trap that can only be broken in an acknowledgment that life does involve pain and suffering. Until I came to accept this truth I could never be happy. I have only been happy in these years since I have accepted both laughter and tears.

The immense pain I felt in the aftermath of my marriage relationship produced the response which stated, 'I will never allow anyone else into my life in a way that allows me ever to be hurt.' But at the same time I wanted mature friendship, for that was the only really satisfactory way to live. If I loved I would cry; if I did not love I would not cry. Isolation appeared to defer pain but then I had the pain of never knowing the big feelings of life – joy or sorrow. It had been a sterile existence. My new life held both joy and pain.

The very nature of life is that it changes as it grows, and so our Fisherfolk family changed. Some of the people with whom I had first experienced 'belonging to' as one family moved to establish Community of Celebration life in Scotland and to work within the church there. They included Virginia, John and Margo and their children. We knew *why* we were changing – it was not a denial of friendships, yet it was a very bleak time to me. I felt again as if I were living through the old marriage breakdown. I had loved, now I cried. Jacqueline cried too, for her good friend Martha was moving.

Not everyone moved to Scotland. Jon and Sylvia were standing with me as we waved goodbye to those going north. As I waved goodbye to the Farras – some really close friends, I realized that it would be quite a while before we saw each other again. By then baby Susann would not even know us any more. I was in tears and found that Jon put his arm round me, unembarrassed by my tears. This was our life as much as the laughter was. Through days that were as painful to me as any I had ever experienced, I found I had friends who offered love and care all the time. I was neither isolated nor lonely in my grief.

When John left for Scotland his words to me were, 'Don't stop loving.' Finding my grief understood and accepted by my friends, I found I was able to choose to continue in openness and trust, not rebuilding my old protective shell.

I know that when I stop living wholeheartedly, with

children and adults, then I will not laugh very much, nor will I cry so often either.

Should I have protected Jacqueline from such experiences? Though I was tempted to make life comfortable for her, I saw something better. One year I had given her a carpentry set for Christmas. I encouraged her to hammer in the nails, even though she hit her fingers sometimes. I would have failed her if I had taken away the hammer or tried to do it for her. I could neither protect Jacqueline from the pain of being alive, nor should I try to. If I had allowed her to learn that life is both the good days and the bad ones, I would be glad.

We found that our friendships survived the move. These same people are still my friends and the relationships were not destroyed. I am glad that these experiences left Jacqueline unconvinced by romantic ideas of living happily ever after. I am glad that she thinks it more important that we each live with integrity.

Jodi and I wrote a song together:

> Don't hide away your grief
>   in such dark and lonely places.
> Don't waste away your tears
>   but in weeping share your life.
>
> For I would like to cry with you,
> To share your deepest sorrow,
> To be within your weariness
> And wake with you tomorrow.
>
> We'll walk beneath the shadow
>   and the balm of weeping willows
> Where cool refreshing water
>   laps gently at our side.

I'll wait with you till morning
    has touched on every leaf tip,
And the glow of dawning sunlight
    is shining in the sky.

For I would like to laugh with you
    and teach you that delight
Can walk beside deep waters
    and compassion is their child.

That was not the only song we wrote together. The focus of our life was worshipping God. That was what brought us together and kept us going. I did not think of myself as being very 'religious' but at the same time my life was built around my experience of God. It is easy for one person to be swept away by emotions or even fantasy about God. This experience found perspective in our worship and daily life together. Conversation with others was a good way to sift the real from the unreal. Living faithfully in obedience to God was most expressed in the Eucharist services (Communion), for it is in this service that the church has for two thousand years re-enacted Jesus Christ's sacrifice of his own life and in obedience to him will continue to celebrate this till he returns.

Often over the previous two or three years I had put my private thoughts into poetry. As I got to know Jodi and our friendship grew, so we began to talk about those sorts of thought that I put in my writing, that Jodi also put into music. Out of this came our songs. It was lovely to hear my words with the kind of music I would like to write if I were a musician. In worship I found a soul-friend. We wrote, 'On Tiptoe'.

I walk with you, my children, through
    valleys filled with gloom,
In echoes of the starlight and shadows
    of the moon;

In the whispers of the night wind are
    gentle words for you,
To touch you and assure you it's my
    world you're walking through.

I made the mottled stickle-back to
    hide in crystal streams,
The staring owl to scan the night, the
    candle's gentle beams.
I made the silly camel to roam the
    desert sands,
But you I made, my children, to walk
    and hold my hand.

If life were filled with bubbles, they'd
    glisten and they'd burst.
If life were filled with jewels they'd
    line a rich man's purse.
But life is filled with water that flows
    from depths of love,
It flows to fill your weariness with
    blessings from above.

My love for you, my children, puts
    rainbows in your hands,
Born of clouded sorrows in a sunburst
    morning land;
They arch above the smiling eyes
    where tears can still be seen
And adorn with gentle trembling
    touch the bride who is my own.

It summed up for me that God's love is not a disembodied
emotional trip but is found in the real loving friendship
of God's people. Friends that stick together through the
hard times are friends indeed. Jodi and I both knew it and
still do.

I had not found a way to be rid of all my limitations, weaknesses and inabilities. I still find there are times of despair and of disillusionment, but I have managed to be less self-rejecting about them. In any case, if I were to attempt to become perfect, whose perfection would it be – mine or someone else's? In the meantime I want to live with every ounce I can and I want others to as well.

Other people's weaknesses, or at least those I saw as weaknesses, were often irritating to me. I used to try to avoid them. In a big family they are unavoidable, as are some conflicts. Learning to stay friends through the conflict and through the irritations require faithfulness to one another and in the end we are all probably more accepting of differences between us. As we continued faithful to our friends we all grew.

I realized that I did not want a 'perfect' way for Jacqueline's life. Rather I wanted her to enjoy life through faithfulness and hope in her friendships, having learned how to get through the hard times together. I hoped she was learning creative problem-solving, not building up dreams of a Utopia.

Jacqueline and I were free to believe in friendship. A broken marriage and single parenthood were not the beginning of the end; it was the end of one chapter and the beginning of a new and different one. Perhaps it is not the course I would have chosen, but nevertheless it is a good one.

11

A Larger Family

In all these years as a single parent what has been the result of my involvement in the church? I have talked of the encouragement it was to be among friends who were Christians. But I did not always find the institutional church to be so kind. While many individuals were such good friends, the organization to which they belonged was not. Being a single parent was a non-starter. Of course, my experience is some years ago now, and attitudes and laws – both in society and in the church – are changing. I hope that other people's experience may have been different.

The Community of Celebration was a new kind of church. My experience of life had included enough powerlessness for me to know what it is to be a puppet, dangled and pushed around by people and circumstances. It was a remarkably different system in the Community. Women were people. For example, Virginia was a very gifted leader and as such was accepted, along with other women, among the 'elders' – the leadership team. In a variety of aspects of life, at home and in business, individual 'gifts' were given room for expression. It did not matter whether that talent was shown by a man or a woman. Here were people who were unafraid of women in leadership.

In contrast, I remember talking some years ago to a friend who was later ordained to the priesthood. I was struggling to come to terms with what it meant for me to be a leader. I shall not forget his advice!

'The trouble is,' he said, 'you should have a man in authority over you. Then your leadership gifts could be worked out through him. You should get married.'

I was furious but I laughed too.

'I should get married? When the church will send me to a registry office for the service? Have you got any other bright ideas?'

That defined the dilemma. You have to be married but the church sees remarriage as a second best. And what a dreadful basis for a marriage that some man, as yet unfound, had to be the leader who expressed *my* gifts in *his* life in the church!

What was the church after all? A forever-changing institution founded in the first century. It has changed much with the times and cultures in which it has existed but always it is at heart the gathering of Christians together to be God's people in that place and time, bringing their lives together to worship and serve God. In one part of the New Testament the church is described as not discriminating between Jew and Greek, male and female, slave and free. In general, however, the church in every age has fairly closely paralleled the society in which it lived.

When I looked at the institutionalized church I could see that the decision-making processes and general tenor of life in the contemporary church were determined by a male-orientated structure, and there was an absence of the perspective that women have on life. Men tend to be interested in principles, order, procedure and the headier aspects of theology. Women – as in life – generally tend to be more concerned for personal aspects of caring and helping, with a special concern for children. In some ways men may be seen to be more concerned for justice; and women for mercy. The church needs the expression of both justice and mercy in the way it develops and lives out its life in the world.

Apart from the fact that it is obvious that women do have leadership gifts, male dominance leaves fatherless families on the edge or outside the church. I believe that the different concerns, needs and awarenesses that belong to the single parent should be expressed in the church's leadership groups, and not just secondhand.

Until I joined the Community, I had spent most of my Christian life on the edge of the institutional church. Nowhere was the point made more clearly than by the Mothers' Union, that stalwart champion of and expression of women's life in the church. Their rules excluded me from membership on the grounds of being divorced. Individual members have said, 'Do come along, we don't mind,' but that doesn't really help. It is sad that to the institutional church there have been several 'unforgivable' sins – and one of them is being divorced. Yet there is no way to become undivorced. The marriage has gone, but surely we need a way to show that God's grace is still with us. All the kindness of church members, helpful as it was, did not in the end help this categorization of the single parent as an inferior person. Thank God reform is in the air today.

After the group left us to establish a new Community in Scotland, we re-shaped our life considerably. Until that time I had been working in the office. Then there was a need for someone with appropriate skill and experience to work with young children in the mornings while their older brothers and sisters were at school. It was our own playgroup. I loved the children and enjoyed their company and so I took on this new venture. After a while we talked about my spending some of my time working with the Fisherfolk team as I was skilled in ways appropriate to their work.

The experience of working in the team brought me into a new kind of decision-making. There were no 'parents' on the team, nor was there a boss. For example, two or three people would plan an event or act as a working party. But they were not given special status for this work. A small group might plan this way for the sake of efficiency.

I did not find myself discriminated against on the ground of being a woman or of being a single parent; it was both refreshing and amazing.

We had our disagreements, sometimes quite vehement, but conflict was not resolved by pulling rank or putting down the other person. At times we had to ask someone else from the Community to join our meeting to help throw light on the situation. How could we find a third way through our conflict?

Our lives were changed by discovering that we had the right to be the decision-makers in our own future as well as in daily routines. In all the struggles I had lived through, the lack of money and isolation had hardly given me any choices. Just about everything had been determined by circumstances, patterns of 'normality' and even the expectations of my neighbours. Whether I liked it or not, I had been in the rat-race, along with everyone else and, like a rat in a hopeless maze, I had found neither a solution nor relief.

Now, by the way life was ordered, I could be a whole person. Even though I was both female and a single parent, I was accepted as a peer among the community members. This was a new kind of church.

The experience of travelling with the team showed me new aspects of myself. I found I enjoyed the sense of adventure and challenge. It was an opportunity to develop communication skills, to lead workshops and seminars, to teach and lead worship and to help churches and groups re-evaluate and freshen up their own worship services. Over the years I was asked more and more to talk about children and their part in the church and wrote teaching courses and workshops to help adults and children to learn and worship together.

On my travels I made many new friends. I never failed to be surprised by the fact that people knew who I was because I was identified with the Fisherfolk. It was like someone saying, 'Ah, you're one of the Durran family.' We had a community family identity.

From that time I knew I could never again accept life complacently – accepting the violation of my own or other people's rights to be treated as responsible adults. I found that I had the right to challenge circumstances and prejudices – to question the *status quo*. I am curious and inquisitive and I like to unfold and examine the patterns of life, like turning a kaleidoscope. But I know now that when I find problems I have the right and the will to look for change. That's true whether I'm considering our family life or the society in which we live.

My experience brought into focus some big questions. Can adventurous people who want to discover new horizons belong to the church? Such horizons may not have existed a generation ago so old patterns and rules may have to change to include a new generation. Twenty years ago the church felt morally superior to the single parent, and was very comfortable maintaining that position. Can the church today find a way to offer forgiveness? May the sinner be saved by grace?

When Jacqueline and I came to live among the Fisherfolk family we found ourselves among Christians who were ready and determined to answer such questions. They were completely involved with the church and at the same time ready to change and grow. They were not guardians of the *status quo*. They were a Christian family who were building the structures of its life around its members, not requiring them to conform themselves to a predetermined calcified structure.

This gives me hope for the church. This way, Christians can be both freer and more responsible in their friendship and family life. They can include those people who might otherwise be on the edge or excluded. I hope that the antiquated forms of church institution will be affected for change by this new generation of members who are more caring, more accepting and more ready to forgive, and who offer a share in power, in freedom and equality.

In our family Jacqueline had always been encouraged to look outwards, to tackle new challenges and to be adventurous. When we were having supper one evening, she said to me, 'Mum,' she sounded very serious, 'do you know? You have never stopped me doing anything I have wanted to do. I don't mean when I was naughty or anything of that kind, but new things. You helped me to try so I could find out for myself what I wanted to do and what I could do. For several days I have been meaning to tell you.'

I gulped. I was glad to know. This was what I had wanted to offer Jacqueline in her growing up but I had not yet stopped to assess whether I had really managed to do it.

This poses more questions. When many young people of Jacqueline's age are coming to terms with their own responsibility for themselves and others, is there room for them to grow in the church? Can the church allow young people to question seriously and to come to their own conclusions? Is there room for discovery and adventure, or does the church see itself as the guardian of the *status quo*? Can young people of both sexes grow into adults who carry responsibility and leadership in a new generation? Churches sometimes seem to eye the life of young adults with disapproval or mild tolerance while giving them no place in the existing power structures.

While I worked on the Fisherfolk team, travelling away from home, Jacqueline stayed at home with our good friend Sylvia. On our tours, we visited hundreds of churches and met thousands of people, sharing in their worship. After visiting cities and villages, large and small towns, and churches of all denominations, it was apparent that the church is quite middle-class. In many cases when working people join a church they rapidly become not only Christian, but middle-class.

Given that some values of the middle-class church are admirable – like discouraging smoking and violence, for example – I am sure that middle-class values are generally no more godly than working-class ones.

In effect, the present 'Christianization' programme – what happens to people when they become Christians – tends to take working-class people out of the local community and transfer them into a middle-class one. Unfortunately, they do not do so well in it as the middle-class colleagues who were born to it. Certainly, I was fooled by the system for a long time. Now I realize that a lot of the qualities of the ordinary working people among whom I grew up are good and positive. In one way I found the working-class community to be the more forgiving of single parenthood, more accepting of the family as just another family. In fact, the strength of the traditional working-class community in its mercy and forgiveness of its members would be a gift to the church, if there was room to receive it.

The church, if it has any great meaning, is a family that follows Jesus. That family lives together and has fun together; it is a community which accepts *all* its members with all their different backgrounds and cultures and which affirms none above the other. The church should have no class systems.

I recently visited an inner-city church on a Saturday. From a fifth-floor balcony a man in flannels and braces watched with curiosity the activity in the church ground below. Someone had brought a football, and some men were playing with a group of children. They laughed and shouted a great deal. There was a picnic lunch spread out on the grass and lots more people were gathered there chatting. Toddlers were climbing over the old tombstones.

My friends who are the leaders in that church realized that their growth would come through what they made of life together, through their becoming a kind of local community family in which they and others could feel at home. In such a neighbourhood different groups of people meeting separately – in Sunday School or Youth Group – would never meet and get to know the other members of the church, and perhaps not even recognize them in the street. A primary step was to abandon separate groups, divided by age or sex or whatever, and all meet together on Sunday mornings for worship, and really become a family together.

I enjoy going to visit that church. Around the church building are high-rise flats, broken windows and all the features of urban decay. The area has little social pride. But these people come together in mutual acceptance, receiving each person and each family as they are. There is a kind of gospel message which says, 'Come and be part of our family, we would like to have you with us.' The social and cultural requirements which so often seem necessary for active involvement in church life do not apply here.

When the life and structures of the church are built around being a family together, such as we experienced in the Community of Celebration, then I have hope for myself and Jacqueline, and other single-parent families.

12

A Travelling Parent

When I became involved with the travelling team of the Fisherfolk Jacqueline was thrilled. It meant a change in our life-style. The pattern of our time together changed and we had our low as well as high points.

There were decisions to be made. One incident from early on sticks in my mind. School summer holidays were getting closer and Jacqueline was very keen to go to the Community in Scotland and spend some time there with her friends, especially Martha. Our Fisherfolk team had received invitations to run two conferences in the summer break – one in York, the other in Sussex. Should we both be away at the same time? Jacqueline would be first with Virginia and then with Martha's mother. Surely she would be fine. We both went our separate ways and I promised myself I would write quite frequently. I was in York ten days and wrote to Jacqueline twice. Each was a package with a letter, cards and little bits I'd found in the shops that she would like. I wrote to her from Sussex, where I stayed for a week.

I arrived home to find Virginia and others had sent notes to ask why I hadn't contacted Jacqueline or written to her. She had looked out every day for the postman. She had received only one.

Two weeks later the team member who had taken my letters to Jacqueline to post in the town found them in the bottom of his bag. He was extremely apologetic. I gave them to Jacqueline anyway, but it was not quite the same. From then on, I was much more careful about my communication and who took letters to the post!

Whenever it was reasonable and especially if we were not too far from home, Jacqueline and other children of team members joined in the day conferences or workshops we were leading. We wrote new plays and songs for special occasions. For Christmas we prepared new materials. I wrote several short scenes to tell the Christmas story through the eyes of the villagers in Bethlehem, as well as the shepherds and kings.

The shepherds bumbled onto the stage – we were in Blandford, Dorset – extremely puzzled about the light in the sky. They stumbled over rocks and into ditches with trying to see what was there. One shepherd at last declared he was sure he was seeing angels. The others shouted him down saying he had had too much whisky that evening. But then they saw the angels too.

The next scene was of a child in Bethlehem trying to persuade her mother to let her go to see the new baby in the stable. Jacqueline played the child. She wheedled and cajoled and promised to be good till at last she was allowed to go.

The three kings were a little more traditional.

Sylvia, Jacqueline and others had come that evening to join with the local church we were visiting. All our children loved to come with us and be identified as our family. Seeing us standing up at the front leading music and speaking and acting in small plays, probably helped them not only to know what we were doing but also to see themselves as part of something bigger than just the ordinary round of everyday tasks.

The following summer many of the children who were over eight years old went on a holiday trip to the north of Scotland. The car journey usually took around eighteen hours. The children went with six adults in two minibuses and one large car – the latter towed a trailer heaped with food, sailing equipment, waterproofs and sleeping bags. They were going to stay in an old church.

It was there that Jacqueline learned to sail and to catch fish for the meals. Lobsters were caught in marked baskets which were dropped down into the bay and then hauled in later. After two weeks of working together, some of them learning to cook for the first time, the whole group set off home again. The plan was to stop off on the return journey to spend a day or two with the Community of Celebration in Scotland, to break the journey and enjoy a reunion with old friends.

While they were there a small crisis arose. Two adults from the community in Scotland needed to travel south quite urgently and so the adults bringing our children home decided to leave two of them in Scotland in order to bring the two adults to England. Jacqueline was chosen because she knew so many people there and it was several days before school started. Anticipating no problems with this arrangement, the vehicles set out, leaving Jacqueline and one of the teenagers behind, and someone phoned me later in the day to tell me what was happening.

Nobody had realized that the situation had created a considerable problem. Thirty-six hours later I was due to be in Ireland. Our original plan had meant I would see Jacqueline before I left. This was to be the Fisherfolk's first visit to Ireland. While visitors to Ireland really were quite safe, Jacqueline had heard and seen enough on the news to be very worried that I would be injured or killed while away. This meant that we had talked it over at length when we first took the decision to go.

I knew Jacqueline would be very upset to return home two days late and find I had already left for Ireland without her seeing me, so I talked to her and Virginia in Scotland on the phone. Virginia, who was able to see the whole thing in its context, volunteered to drive Jacqueline to Glasgow airport and get her on a plane south. I would pick her up at Heathrow.

At Heathrow Airport, Jacqueline was delighted to see

me. She was escorted off the plane by the hostess who had looked after her on the flight. She was full of stories of what it meant to catch a plane, her first ever. To her it was a great adventure. She was well settled at home with Sylvia and the rest of the household before I left for Ireland.

On our return we drove home through the night from the ferry which landed at Fishguard in South Wales. We arrived at our house just in time for me to take Jacqueline to school. It was her first day at the comprehensive school. We were delighted.

Another time the travelling team was going to Cornwall for ten days and we decided to take the whole household with us. Jon and Sylvia's children came as well as Jacqueline. We travelled in a Bedford minibus. It had nine seats and a space behind for props, equipment and luggage. There was very little space left over when we all crammed in. We had to leave Edgar with friends; he would have been impossible. He liked to spread out while travelling, moving round and round to get comfortable.

We arrived in Truro in the late afternoon. The children had had enough and were a bit grumpy. Jon and Sylvia and their children were staying in a caravan, like real holiday-makers. Jacqueline and I, with another team member, were staying in a convent.

Jacqueline made friends with Sister Rosemary immediately. I was a little worried that the kind of serenity I associated with convents would be too disturbed by Jacqueline's active personality. I wondered whether mealtimes would be silent, because I knew Jacqueline would chatter away happily. But Sister Rosemary settled my worries – I had not even voiced them before it became obvious that the nuns enjoyed having children around.

When we weren't working during that week, we went off to the beach and on outings with the children. One afternoon they were fascinated as we drove across a deserted stretch of countryside to see great ships 'parked' on the land. Only when we got very close to them did the children see what we already knew. In Cornwall there are some very narrow, deep river valleys, running down to the sea like Norwegian fjords. An oil company had moored their out-of-use ocean-going tankers here. At night, they were even lit up. The tiny ferry taking us across the river seemed like a toy boat next to those towering giants.

Before we left Cornwall Sister Rosemary took Jacqueline around the convent, showing her all kinds of unusual things. Under a sink in the laundry room were some lumps of soap that had been hand-made by the nuns during the last War when there had been shortages. Jacqueline gratefully received a couple of the browny-green lumps as souvenirs of her visit.

After an open-air celebration – a time of worship in song, with dance and drama – we left Cornwall. It was about 10 p.m. and it was beginning to get dark. We had decided to travel home overnight while all the children were asleep. It was fine until we were two hours' journey from home, and the minibus broke down. From the clanks and bangs at the final moment, the problem sounded serious! We found ourselves stranded in the middle of nowhere with several children who would soon wake up demanding breakfast.

Eventually we found a phone and rang the Community. We woke some very surprised people who came to fetch us. We saw the dawn together before were eventually picked up, which helped considerably through the waiting. We left some of the team with the bus and they arrived home a day later after sorting out the repairs needed.

The effect of my new working life – of travelling – had been that Jacqueline and I experienced how effectively a community can be a family. While our own relationship was always the most significant one for both of us, I was not the person who met all Jacqueline's needs. Any 'nuclear' family – parent(s) and children – in the Community found that the care and nurture of children was a community family concern. A household such as ours looked after the needs of *all* our children, without preferences. Going away for a weekend was not like leaving Jacqueline at boarding school, but like leaving her with relatives in her own home, and life carried on just the same.

By the late seventies we began to concentrate more on inviting people to conferences on our premises, than on travelling so much. This meant that our whole community could be involved and be together in what we were doing. So people came and camped on our field and we ran a conference programme and all our children could join in as well.

I began to specialize in the work with the children and to structure programmes to give us many opportunities for discovery and creativity.

The conference programmes were geared to children as much as to adults. I remember one year a leader working with Jacqueline's age-group had asked the children to work on some plays with a moral. The plays were then shown to all the adults at the conference. As Jacqueline's group climbed on to the stage, I had no idea what to expect. They had found preparing their play so funny that they were already almost overwhelmed with giggles. The story went: there was once a short, thin man who wanted to buy an icecream from a van that stopped by the roadside. But he wasn't too careful of the traffic. Jacqueline, now consumed by hysterical laughter which infected everyone, produced the man after he had been run over by a steam-roller. The figure had been cut from a very large roll of card and the man had been reduced to a flattened silhouette, little more than a shadow. The moral of the story was, 'Be careful how you buy icecreams. If there's a steam-roller coming, you might end up like this.' And Jacqueline held the poor victim high so everyone could appreciate the results of such folly.

There was always so much fun – many new people to meet and new friends to enjoy. Our work became a highlight of the school holidays for the children. They loved camping; they loved the programme that was arranged; they enjoyed working with us. All the Community children saw themselves as belonging to one large family that worked together and played together. And during these conferences we saw all ages mixing and caring for one another.

13

New Friends

Travelling with the team brought me into contact with many lone parents.

We pulled in at The Vicarage and Jon stuffed the road map back in the cubby-hole. 'Well, we made it in good time.' The vicar came out of his door, with a beaming smile and welcoming words.

We stretched, stiff from sitting too long.

'Come in and have a cup of tea. My wife's got the kettle on. Then afterwards we can go over our plans and I'll direct you to the houses where you are staying.'

Tea, biscuits and talk.

'Two of you are staying with a family near the station and two with Shelley...'

The vicar, it seemed, thought it might be a little hard for Shelley to manage to have people to stay but it was obvious that she had really wanted some of us to go there.

We wondered what we would find. We might not want to stay there.

The directions took us to a terraced house, its door opening right onto the pavement. From the outside it looked like all the others. We shrugged and rang the bell. There was a flurry of sound, pounding feet, and a young boy opened the door. Then he was overcome with shyness.

'Hello. Is this Shelley's house? The vicar sent us here.'

He was saved from answering for Shelley herself appeared. 'Oh, do come in. Peter, bring them in the kitchen. It's nice and warm in there.'

We met the family then – Shelley and three children.

'I hope you won't mind, things are a little sparse, but I did want you to come,' she said.

Over the next two days we heard more of Shelley's story. There were two boys and a girl – Shelley's husband had left some three years before. Even before the time he left there was little spare money but they had been gradually saving for things they specially wanted, such as a Welsh dresser, making do with rather scruffy cast-offs from others till they could get what they really wanted. Since he left, Shelley had made do with the cast-offs. They were a happy family and had lots of fun together. There was no television – they couldn't afford it.

At some point in the weekend Shelley realized that I was also a lone parent. She gave me a funny look and was quiet for a while. It was one of those strange recognitions that go deeper than words. People in the church saw Shelley as a little over-anxious, trying a little too hard, a bit more afraid than necessary. When she caught my eye, Shelley realized I lived with the same inner pressures, and we understood one another.

Shelley was actually taking herself and her family through their growing up, with the normal fears of lone parents. 'I cannot make it, the ends don't meet. But I will do it. I feel like giving up, but I have no choice. I will go on.' I never wanted to offer her sympathy, though there was room for it, because I'd found myself that sympathy ate cracks in the determination to go on. A person cannot cry and grit their teeth at the same time. Crying is relaxing and coping requires constant driving from within, like running a marathon.

Each summer Shelley and the children moved upstairs and slept in the loft so that holiday-makers could rent the rest of the house. Shelley gave them breakfast and an evening meal. The children were getting used to the arrangement and were just old enough to realize that it resulted in financial gain.

Back at home we came across more family problems. Someone was complaining about a boy who came onto the local Caravan Park every day. As it was private property, he should not have been there. But every day he came back, sat in the lounge and watched television, bought a pie for lunch, and spent the rest of his time riding round on his bike. He was a bit of a nuisance – cheeky and a little rebellious – and about eleven years old.

One of the staff eventually asked him, 'Why do you keep coming here? Why don't you just watch your own television at home?'

'I can't,' he answered. 'Mum's out at work so she locks me out. She says I'm not safe in the house on my own. She says I must find somewhere to go. When she gets home, I go back then.'

He was just one of the thousands of children of lone parents who either have their own key and fend for themselves in the school holidays, or are locked out as this boy was, for their own safety.

Another lone parent was Andrew, left by his wife with three small children, the youngest just a couple of months old. He had had two weeks off work when it first happened – he had a sympathetic boss. But he was absolutely numb with shock and months later was still trying to cope with his grief. Members of the church had the baby during the day, the middle child – a boy – was at a nursery and the oldest was at school.

The older children suffered the change badly. John, the eldest, was very close to his father and used to sit down with him and say, 'I made Mummy go. I want to make her come back. I made Mummy go.'

'No, it's not your fault Mummy left,' Andrew assured him.

'Whose fault is it? I didn't want her to go.'

They had cried together more than once but John was gradually beginning to settle in his new life.

His younger brother, though, could not put his questions into words. He began to misbehave to extremes, throwing tantrums, screaming and running frantically. He fought all authority, struggled against anyone who picked him up.

Andrew was hesitant but did the only thing that came to mind – that was to hold his son until he stopped struggling and kicking, until he would receive affection. John kept telling his brother, 'It's all right, it's not your fault.' But his brother was too disturbed to hear.

The church concerned asked me to talk to them about single parents because they wanted to help Andrew. Some members were already working together to help with the baby and some household chores. But every day Andrew got up early, got the boys ready for school, packed the baby's bag and pram and delivered all three to various friends who would take them to school with their own children. Then he went off to work. In the evening he reversed the process, getting them all home, cooking a meal, sorting out baths, stories and bedtime prayers. Then as they settled he washed up and cleared up the toys and clothes, packed lunches for the next day, gave the baby a last bottle for the night and fell into bed. A holiday from work meant that all three children were with him all the time.

It was impossible. The church members could see Andrew's weariness and grief. 'What can we do?' they asked. They were doing all that could be done by helping and by carrying the load of practical chores and cares. No one could change the circumstances and, as long as they continued to help the family, they would have to work within the circumstances with Andrew. Friendship is both healing and encouraging. This family would make it through.

I am reminded of what might seem a very minor incident.

Janet rang me up. 'Maggie, I was thinking of getting some Italian cheese for a recipe I want to do tomorrow

116

night. Susan said you had some Mozarrella. Is there any chance I could buy three ounces from you?'

'You can have three ounces, there's no need to pay for it.'

One parent with one toddler would want only a little cheese, but who dares go into a shop to ask for only three ounces of something? I remember the dread of watching shop assistants cut cheese and offer it to me – two ounces more than I had asked for. For a special cheese I would calculate to the last penny to see if I could afford it. I could hardly go two ounces over. While it's difficult in a shop, you can ask friends.

Lone parents have to struggle between keeping within a budget and self-respect. They want to feel normal – able to shrug off the extra pennies – yet to me it used to feel like an actual weight on my shoulders, dragging at me and making me feel sick.

When I meet lone parents asking for help I know they have already struggled with wanting to cope alone, to make life work. But even those who have not asked need the help, especially if they are living on Supplementary Benefit. When they do not ask I offer only very lightly because self-respect keeps their head up. I'd hate to suggest in any way that I doubted their ability to cope. When they do ask it reminds me of the words of Jesus: 'If someone asks for your coat, give him your cloak also.' I don't have much and neither do they, but if we help one another we'll both do better.

Another person I met on my travels was Anne. Her husband had been a curate. She had built her whole life around him, adapting to his life and work as a vicar's wife has to. Then he left her for a new partner – another member of the church, who was also married. From that point onwards, Anne had to rebuild her life.

The vicar of the church where her husband had been training was extremely helpful. As a curate is only located

117

in a church for a couple of years for training, Anne would not usually have expected to stay there. But Anne and her small son – David – were encouraged to stay and to establish a life of their own. Festivals and holidays were hardest. At Christmas, Anne and David often joined with the lively family at the Vicarage for the celebrations and Christmas fare.

Some of the church members began organizing group holidays – camping – so again Anne and David had a place to belong which was bigger than just the two of them. Through the constant care and friendship of a few individuals in the church, Anne was gradually able to get her life in order, find her own house and start a mortgage. She was able to re-establish self-respect and, after the trauma of becoming a lone parent, was in many ways more self-assured, more self-sufficient than she had ever been.

Of all the lone parents I met, perhaps the hardest to talk to was a woman in her mid-thirties who approached me at a conference. I do not remember her name. Her two teenage children were comfortably settled in boarding school and she had a beautiful home in an affluent area in the West Country. Her husband was alcoholic. Drinking-bouts made him angry and violent. He often beat her. But when she left him he became pitiful, crying and pleading with her. At some level she still loved him – at least she saw he needed her. She wanted to leave again, for she was afraid of the violence and abuse, but she was also afraid that if she did, life for her and the children would be squalid and poor. She was trapped by her life-style as well as by the emotional ties with her husband. As she spoke, she seemed to be entirely in two minds. I think she was not exaggerating the violence but was afraid of having no one to depend on for money and living.

I gave her the names of organizations that would help if she did leave and I realized that there are many women like her, trapped because they closed their career options years before to raise children. It takes considerable determination to open them again and fend for the family oneself.

More and more I met churches and groups who wanted to care for and encourage the lone parents among them. It was hard for them to realize that the basis of society had changed so much and that church structures and social structures could no longer be built on traditional models – the husband at work, wife at home in the day. Instead new ways must be found to structure the church or many of the people who most want – and need – a larger family to belong to, will be kept on the margin. Just as when I was teaching I did not fit in with what the church provided for women – Young Wives or Mothers' Union – so it seemed that many lone parents had too few resources to make it in a structure designed around the two-parent model. Maybe it was time for a different model – one that could include everyone. Maybe the Community of Celebration really had something to say through its family life which effectively included so many different people.

14

Into the World

When she was in her early teens Jacqueline asked if I would buy her a car when she reached eighteen.

'No. I'm sorry, I won't,' I said.

Jacqueline then pointed out an eighteen-year-old who had a car – someone she knew well.

'We don't have enough money and probably won't by the time you're eighteen, either,' I replied. 'But if I have a car then I expect you can drive it.'

The problem was not one that single parents are alone in facing. It's easy for us all to get the message from society that if we *really* loved our children, then we would give them everything.

Throughout Jacqueline's life it was a priority to let her know that I loved her and that she belonged and I was glad she was there, even when we had no money. I wanted her to know that whatever the size of Christmas and birthday presents, they all expressed my love, and that the size or value was not a direct measure of how much I loved her.

As far as I am concerned, life is not about accumulating wealth, but I want an income that is adequately above the bread line to avoid the grinding stress that comes from worrying about heating bills and food prices. But more than that I am not too worried.

Jacqueline went to comprehensive schools where they set the colour for uniforms but not the style. In other types of school – grammar school, for instance – the cost of uniforms can be incredibly high and way above the pocket of ordinary people. Poorer people are not second class! Material wealth and 'keeping up with the Joneses' is cruel to those who do not have that much money. After all, it is not as if anyone is any better as a person for all their possessions, but sometimes those people tend to look down on others who lack wealth and possessions.

In a Sunday School teachers' meeting one day we talked about this issue because many parents found it an undercurrent of conversation, even while mothers were waiting outside the school gates for the children to come out. There was a kind of general expectation of an 'acceptable' amount to spend on children. One mother reported getting funny looks because she and her husband spent a lot on one of their children; others felt put down that they had not spent as much.

Sometimes I think our family has been better off for having less money! We did not even have enough to join the race, and we had to work things out for ourselves. I remember Jacqueline's excitement one Christmas when she was only five years old. Some friends of ours gave her a beautiful set of poster paints and a drawing-book. She spent most of the day at work with these and then used them many times over the next couple of years. I remember some other friends – a family who had been sent some money as a Christmas gift. They gave some of it to me to buy Jacqueline a present – I was so overwhelmed by their love that I cried.

I frequently saw in myself and other single parents a great tendency to be over-protective. There was no one else to say: 'You're fussing too much about nothing.' Sometimes I had a picture before me of a middle-aged man still living at home and his mother still treating him as a child, checking he had a hankie in his pocket. I dreaded to think of us getting like that.

It felt an enormous risk to release my control of Jacqueline and my protection of her. I was immensely afraid of letting her find her own way in life.

Our house was several miles from the school, and children

had to be taken there by car or ride bikes. I was always rather relieved to take Jacqueline by car, even though one of our cars was so old that she hid behind the seat if she thought anyone she knew might see her! Then, when she changed school at eleven years and began at the comprehensive school, there were no other children going in her direction and so lifts became complicated. Several people suggested she should ride her bike but I was afraid for her safety, even though many children her age rode to school. It was very hard to overcome my fear but eventually I decided it was a good idea. I knew I would have to try to be less protective.

One day a child in Jacqueline's class was critically injured at a junction which Jacqueline had to cross each day. One of our household had been there almost immediately after the crash and had helped until the ambulance came. The girl had turned across in front of a fast-moving car, while talking to a friend.

Two days later on another street I saw another child do an almost identical thing, and saw her tumbling from the bonnet of the vehicle. I rushed from my car, normally terrified by even the sight of blood. A crowd had gathered and they were all just looking at the girl lying in the road. The driver, who had hit her, was hunched over the steering wheel in shock. I had never done any first aid but I had read bits in magazines, so I sent a man to a local house to phone the ambulance and get a blanket. I could see a great bruise forming on the girl's head and was relieved when she moved and began to try to talk – very incoherently. A bystander told me where she lived and someone fetched her mother. She could not cope with the situation of being close to the child, so I found myself talking to the girl and reassuring her until the ambulance arrived and capable hands took over.

I stood by the roadside, watching the ambulance drive off. The crowd dispersed and the traffic was beginning to flow normally. I was amazed to find I was more calm and less scared than I had imagined I could be in such circumstances. While the horror of both situations had not diminished, I found that my fear of accidents had. I still worried about Jacqueline and whether she was riding with more care than these two children had but some deeper fear had somehow been resolved through these peculiar circumstances.

It was hard for me not to be afraid that something would diabolically affect Jacqueline's life. Years before it had been a regular nightmare – something awful had happened to Jacqueline! I grew to realize that when I was already depressed, then I became extremely afraid for Jacqueline. When I felt okay myself, then I was relatively unafraid for her. So the problem was not that Jacqueline was particularly unsafe or in danger, but that I was depressed. I worked out that if on the days that I felt quite reasonable I considered the way Jacqueline rode her bike or travelled or took part in sports, then I could be assured of her safety. On days that I felt discouraged, I learned to trust the decisions I had already made and not make any new ones.

I wanted to learn to set Jacqueline free to live adventurously if she wanted to, and not to control her life with *my* difficult feelings. So I had to deal with my feelings. The accident I had seen and the more serious one I had not seen brought my feelings right to the surface where I found I had to sort them out and deal with them.

On a lighter note, but not less important for that, it was sometimes a struggle to let go in the areas of personal choice – in shoes and clothing.

'Mum, I've seen the shoes I want for school.'

'What are they like?'

'They are brown leather and – '

'How high are the heels?'

Every time we bought school shoes we had the same

conversation – the problem was always the height of the heels. Until Jacqueline was ten we were fine buying her shoes together. From then on the battle happened regularly. I always tried to get her to have the lower heels; she wanted higher. I could not imagine anyone wanting to rush around school all day in three-inch heels. She was convinced that anything less would make her look a fool in front of all her friends.

Once we got to the shop the brown ones were far too high, but I somehow let myself be persuaded. Later I discovered that Jacqueline was wearing them to go to school and on her arrival was changing into her tennis shoes for the rest of the day. My only comfort was that at least she was not wearing those heels all day, and in the circumstances tennis shoes were probably preferable. After that I gave her the money and let her buy her own shoes. She always bought flat ones.

A couple of years later I found myself starting to tell her what to buy but was quickly stopped. I apologized. If I was going to trust her to buy shoes then I must trust and let her go shopping without my interference. If she wanted my advice she would ask for it.

Teens are hard years for parents and children! Long after Jacqueline was able to make responsible decisions I found myself automatically trying to tell her what to do. I found that I could be provoking her into making negative choices just to prove she had the right to decide. The more I allowed her to be responsible, the more she was. After a while she was more helpful to me in her responses.

In some ways I made life hard for Jacqueline by making her aware of the meaning of responsibility for herself. At sixteen one of Jacqueline's teachers grumbled about her hairstyle, saying it was unsuitable for school. Jacqueline was perturbed and started to question the school's right to impose its likes and dislikes about a personal matter such as hairstyle. In the course of the conversation, which in the end turned out quite well, Jacqueline told the teacher that, rather than being against the way her hair was styled, it was her mother who had cut it that way in the first place.

All that both Jacqueline and the teacher had said in the conversation was true. I had cut Jacqueline's hair the way she wanted it and for years she had chosen her own hairstyle. A hairstyle does seem to be a question of personal choice, but Jacqueline herself had to choose whether to make an issue of her rights or to acknowledge that only the school could give her the education she wanted. She had to decide whether it might be necessary to conform at that stage in order to get what she wanted, and accept some infringements of personal rights. It was Jacqueline's choice. She adapted her hairstyle.

There is a knife-edge between being protective on one hand or domineering on the other. There is a narrow line between freedom to be yourself and responsibility to others, with an acknowledgment of the order of society. Some rules are there to be challenged; many are not. How does a person decide which is which? I did not want to bring Jacqueline up in an egoism, a self-centred attitude, that let her believe that the world should be manipulated and changed to suit her viewpoint. Yet I wanted her to know she has a right to her viewpoint, alongside all the other viewpoints.

One day I overheard an acquaintance of ours debating with Jacqueline the question of whether she believed in God. He seemed upset that Jacqueline did not give a decisive answer and became frustrated with her position, dismissing it as not possible, and trying to convince her with Bible verses. Jacqueline was good in the conversation, not allowing herself to be pressurized to come to a conclusion that she was not really ready to make.

I realized that the adult involved in the conversation was unaware of a teenager's need to sift through the values and attitudes, the principles of the family's life, in order to understand and take responsibility for her own views. This process takes time and with Jacqueline has involved taking up attitudes that were alien to me. But it was only by trying them out that Jacqueline discovered what she wanted to adopt. At one time Jacqueline's history teacher was worried because Jacqueline began to read biographies of Hitler, with interest, and was asking questions about whether he could have been right. As so many people did believe Hitler was right – at the time – and blindly followed him, I thought Jacqueline should be able to discover for herself why Nazism should or should not be accepted. This would mean that in her own life in the future she would more readily discern the dangers of all sorts of political positions.

For example, when I was at school I was convinced for a while by South African friends that apartheid was fair and just, and what everyone in South Africa really wanted. After a time I grew out of that position. I wanted to give Jacqueline opportunity to think such issues through for herself. It was she who discouraged me from banking with a certain High Street bank for political reasons. What Jacqueline said was reasonable and I came to agree with her. I changed my bank.

One aspect of her growing social consciousness alerted me to the fact that though I saw good causes and ways of being different, I tended to do nothing. Maybe it was complacency or even laziness. When South African black people encouraged financial embargo, was I going to buy Cape fruit? Jacqueline's youth made her an activist who required integrity – that was a healthy influence on me. As an adult I had lost the determination to do something with my opinions.

While we were still not keen television viewers, we were both avid newspaper readers. Significant articles were cut out and fixed to the kitchen wall above the telephone. Jacqueline's concerns generated a renewed interest in society around us.

15

An Adventurous Person

Jacqueline, aged eleven, rushed in through the door, saying, 'Mum, I want to go to Cumbrae with Dawn and Wendy.'

These were two fifteen-year-old friends in the Community.

'What do you mean, you want to go with them?'

'They're going to visit the Community in Scotland and I can go with them. They said I can.'

My heart sank. I still saw Jacqueline as a little girl, and here she was wanting to spread her wings. She might get lost.

'How are they getting there?'

'They're going on the coach. They're booking their tickets and I can go with them. They will look after me.'

Dawn and Wendy were very careful teenagers but if they took Jacqueline along what would happen if they got tired of her company or there were problems of some kind?

'We'll go on the coach to London, then get the overnight coach to Glasgow, then get the train to Largs. It will be all right, Mum, really it will.'

In the end, I decided she could go with them, unsure whether I had made the decision because my fears had subsided or because I had really seen the reasonable nature of the request.

The trip went well and Jacqueline phoned from Scotland to say she had arrived safely!

I was beginning to learn to set her free to live adventurously.

Before long, Jacqueline began to go to concerts and discos

with some of her young teenage friends at the local Arts Centre. They planned the details together at school and I was usually asked to transport them one way and another parent would make the return journey. Sometimes there were five or six girls all squashed into our little car. I used to drop them outside the hall where an audience of up to two thousand would gather for the concerts. I worried sometimes that there might be a fight but the girls were really quite safe being taken and collected by parents. If Jacqueline was going to be a bit late home it was usually when I was fetching her anyway or other times I would wait up until she arrived home.

Then as a sixteen-year-old she began to go out with friends who were old enough to be car owners and so I no longer controlled the situation through giving lifts. Living in the middle of the country meant that there had been no going out unless she had been taken, so Jacqueline and I had never had to agree a curfew, a time to be in, it had never been necessary. How could I begin to make hard and fast rules where there had been none before?

Jacqueline was long past the stage when rules were given and kept 'because I said you must!' She wanted to understand the basis for the rule. Was it reasonable to set a time and, if so, what? I had begun to be concerned that school work was not getting done, with social life becoming so interesting, so Jacqueline and I talked about the problem. Since Jacqueline wanted to go on to further education, she had to do well in her school work so we agreed that, apart from a few special occasions, going out would be a weekend activity. Coming home time was negotiated according to the event. If I was expecting Jacqueline home and for some reason she was delayed, she phoned me.

Jacqueline began to spread her boundaries further. The first step was rather by chance. At school she made friends with Adrien. Together they trailed around the shops and galleries and markets in London on a Saturday. The following school holiday she went to stay with Helen, an architect who lives in North London. For several days Jacqueline browsed around markets, exhibitions, galleries and shops. She was finding London for herself and finding her feet in it. Home she came with a suitcase full of purchases – shoes, a dress, records – and with her clothes in a couple of plastic bags.

When the Rolling Stones came to do a tour of the country, their first in several years, Jacqueline wanted to go but she could only get a ticket for the Leeds concert, about three hundred miles away. Eventually she discovered that Naomi would like to go with her and found someone else who would give them a ride north. Then she found family friends to stay with in Leeds for two nights. Eve, a lone parent, and her son Rupert had been friends of mine for some years. Even so, Jacqueline would not have seen much if another friendly concert-goer hadn't offered her his rucksack to stand on so she could see over the heads of the crowd.

After the concert the buses could not cope with the thousands of people leaving the ground. So Eve and Rupert took their old car across the city through all the traffic to rescue Jacqueline and Naomi, waiting by the roadside.

Bournemouth, our nearest major town, is a centre for illegal drugs. Many young people have drifted here from the towns in the north of the country to enjoy the sandy beaches – being unemployed by the sea is far more attractive than being in the industrial north. And out of their aimlessness has grown a thriving drug trade. Drugs are sold in all the places of entertainment where young people go, as well as in the pubs and many of the schools. As does every parent, I feared the consequences. One fear I had was that Jacqueline's respect for herself was not sufficient to stop her using drugs. But I suppose that if she had not had self-respect she might have found drugs anywhere. Rather than there being a risk that she would get hooked on drugs against her better judgment, there was also the risk that she had not learned good judgment! That risk was also a test for me. Did I really believe she had the sense to look after herself? Whatever my feelings and fears, I knew that I had to take that risk or Jacqueline could never become a responsible adult.

Saturday nights became nights to go to Bournemouth, to clubs. At first Jacqueline had gone with her school friends, depending still on parents for a lift home. Later her friends had cars and she got lifts with them. One of the new friends who often phoned her at home was very involved with drugs. Sometimes she went out with him on Saturdays.

Summer came. She was seventeen and the Stonehenge rock festival came along. Each year this massive structure of ancient standing stones, dating back to the Iron Age, is the location of a rock festival – a rock festival notorious for drugs. Many people go for several weeks, camping in the fields nearby. Jacqueline's friend wanted her to go with him.

I felt untrusting, even silly, asking questions.

'Can you cope with the situations you may get into?'

'I'll tell you what I am worried about. I am worried that you may get swept into something you have not chosen.'

'Look, I would feel better if I knew that you realize you can phone me to fetch you if the situation is impossible.'

She went for a day and a half, taking an old blanket to sleep in overnight. It was Midsummer's Eve. I have never seen Jacqueline look so dirty as when she returned home. Even then she told me she had washed some of the dust off in the sea at Bournemouth.

The friend started taking heroin and she has not seen much of him since.

In these areas were my greatest struggles to free Jacqueline from my protective control so that she could make her own choices. Unless I let her, I was preventing or delaying her

130

becoming an adult in her own right. While it was my responsibility to see that she had a sound basis of self-respect and to help her with anything she felt she could not handle, having done so, whatever her choice, I had to respect her judgment. My fears for her safety, her future, her life, made me want to choose for her, to control her. Only when she made her own choice was her question and mine answered. Yes, she could handle the pressures of Stonehenge and maintain her integrity.

When she made mistakes, I decided, or a judgment that turned out badly, it was not the time for me to take over control, though perhaps I could help sort out the consequences. I found I must never say, 'I told you so,' or 'Don't do that again!' Jacqueline was a responsible person and quite capable of learning from her mistakes without me nagging her. I could only say, 'Is there anything I can do to help?'

I decided I would give a hand, drive a car if someone didn't want to drink and drive, but I would only do it as I am asked, not by taking over. Sometimes I have had to bite my tongue to stop myself saying the 'motherly' thing, being over-protective. Getting Jacqueline through teen years and into adulthood meant this major transfer of responsibility had to happen without me getting in a fuss about it.

At fifteen Jacqueline left the house and moved into the garage. Our house was out in the country, quite a beautiful house, built for an old couple on their retirement thirty years ago. The garage had been built separately, joined to the house only by a partly-roofed pathway. Some years before we lived there, the occupants had changed this garage first to an office, then a guest room. Jacqueline wanted to live in the garage on her own. She began to care for her own laundry. Cleaning her room had been her responsibility for years. After a while, she did ask me to knock on her window in the morning to make sure she was awake.

I worried a lot at first. What if a burglar came, broke in and attacked her? We would never hear from the house. Some time after that, Jacqueline told me she once heard footsteps on the pathway near her window but they went away again.

Ever since Jacqueline was tiny, I had in mind that I wanted her to learn to be independent and self-sufficient in a responsible way. Lots of sixteen-year-olds leave home, find a flat and a job and look after themselves. Even though Jacqueline was still at school, I wanted her to be able to be self-sufficient, if not by sixteen then definitely when she went to college at eighteen. I wanted her to feel confident about it too.

Moving to the garage was a declaration of independence in many ways. Jacqueline still told me if she was going out in the evening and what time she would be in but I did not wait up for her any more. She let herself in and often she and the friends who brought her home drank coffee in the kitchen before they went home. She had to take responsibility for whether she was keeping up with her school work.

My hazy recollection of the fifties is of there being one predominant style for the whole of the younger generation. During the sixties when people had a little more money there was more variation. Now there were many different and acceptable styles, and much more tolerance of personal choice.

Young people like Jacqueline have established for themselves the right to be different from their parents. Similarly, they have established the right to be different from their peer group without being rejected by it. Young people are choosing their own approach to personal ethics, neither indoctrinated by their parents nor forced into a mould by their peers. Their choices are accepted by peers who are today less afraid of differences. Consciousness of self, self-respect and awareness and respect for others have developed in the last twenty years, even though there are pressures put upon us by the media to conform to a certain pattern.

Despite my fears and hesitations, Jacqueline, as do all teenagers, had had to discover her identity apart from me and become a person in her own right. Our relationship had to provide a few safeguards and a safe foundation for her growth, but my role as mother, and father, had to go through a metamorphosis. I found that I had to change from day to day. I had to adjust drastically. If I had failed to do so and tried to dominate Jacqueline, keeping her a child, our relationship would have broken down.

At first Jacqueline got furiously angry with me. She shouted and stamped and raged.

A friend said to me, 'How can you let her speak to you that way? It is absolutely terrible. You must stop her.'

I hesitated, doubting the wisdom of the advice.

Then the mother of another teenager said, 'I think she is frustrated with life, she has to say it to someone.'

I started to tell Jacqueline sometimes when I was hurt by her angry remarks, but on the whole I was not. We got through it.

There were, too, long periods of depression, when she despaired. She lay in bed till lunchtime, then stayed in the bath till teatime at weekends. But we grew beyond that stage and reached a point where we could talk about almost anything without great difficulty.

Edgar was a faithful friend who grew less aggressive as he grew older. He barked at some people and only got ferocious with one friend who provoked him by growling at him! Edgar ran away around the house every time that friend's car drew up outside.

Edgar's age began to show. He grew very tired on long walks and we sometimes waited while he had a rest. His short legs had to take many more steps than ours. From the time he was nine, Edgar began to visit the vet's with little illnesses more often. As soon as he realized we were turning the car into the road where the surgery was, he used to sink as low as possible in the car. We had always prepared him by putting on his lead, because next we had to tow him along. He dug all four feet into the ground and sat back on his haunches. It was like pulling a vehicle with the wheels locked. We coaxed and edged him along. Woe betide the times his collar was a little loose and slipped over his head – there was no catching him! Once we reached the surgery he behaved quite reasonably as if he knew it was too late to object.

Eventually Sally, a friend who lived with us, and Jacqueline took Edgar to the vet with a bad case of flu. He looked very dreary and obviously had a temperature. The vet gave him a good examination, diagnosed flu and gave him an injection. Edgar felt terrible all evening. He was quite wobbly when he walked and I had to stop him trying to climb the stairs. I gave him a blanket to lie on, and wrapped it around him to help stop his shivering.

When we came downstairs in the morning Edgar had died.

We buried him at the top of the garden under a tree and marked his grave with a white stone. His name was painted on it.

After twelve years of Edgar's company it was strange without him. We missed him wagging his tail when we came home. We had always known if strangers were arriving for Edgar watched from a window on the stair-way and barked at unfamiliar cars pulling in.

At that time I found myself standing at the kitchen sink doing the washing-up and discouraged by the effort of living. I was thinking about Jacqueline and her school work, and, as on many occasions, I was afraid for her and desperately wanted life to work well for her.

I looked out of the window. Beyond the shed and the scramble of blackberry bushes a copse of Scots Pine swayed and shivered in the breeze. Momentarily I forgot my fear, only to have it return with a different perspective. The freshness of those trees spoke to me of the fact that God loves Jacqueline as much as I do, and that I should not try to protect her from the life he has given her.

I was living in transition. For so long I had been Jacqueline's protection and provision. I thought of the days and nights of babyhood; looking out for dangers; teaching her to be wary of cars; showing her how to use tools safely and carefully; introducing her to fun and excitement. I pictured her as a young child, standing outside as the rain fell on her and I had watched her reaction – puzzled and curious – as the drops fell. Or walking wide-eyed on the newly-fallen snow. Rescuing her the day she swallowed the end of her hat ribbon.

Occasionally I had despaired but I had not given up. I could never withdraw and reject her or deny our relationship. All my adult life had been spent making sure that life for Jacqueline was positive, and good for both of us.

Now it was the time of transition, for Jacqueline's boundaries extended beyond the circle of my parenting and control. I was grateful for that sense of God's love.

I had to trust life, that it would be good. Yes, I can see the evil in the world, the disasters, the oppressions, the despair, but, while I may be thought over-optimistic, I believe life is fundamentally good. Despite the fact that cheating exists, most people are trustworthy. Despite there being violence on city streets, most of us are not mugged. There are some accidents and deaths despite our safety precautions, but most of us do arrive safely most of the time. And when that sort of thing happens to us, we are sadder and wiser.

Am I to be reduced to a mean existence, constantly cringeing in fear of this or that, or, having sorrowed and grieved, do I face life again positively? Can I look forward hopefully?

I was oppressed by the message of the media, the news of disasters and despair that fill the television and newspapers. I feared for Jacqueline and wanted to protect her. But I knew that life is out there, too, full of adventure and promise, so I must teach her the safety precautions and let her go. When I realized both that life is good and that God loves Jacqueline I had no need to do this grudgingly or over-fearfully. My feelings were a mixture of excitement and delight, tinged with a little trepidation about the things she would learn the hard way.

16

Adults Together

Just a few days ago Jacqueline and I drove to the village I grew up in. We were visiting relatives to celebrate Jacqueline's eighteenth birthday. She is an adult now.

This Sunday the wind was blustery and cold and, as we drove through Oxford, snow had settled on some of the houses and cars. Once in the country lanes beyond the town a layer of white frosted the fields and verges, the roads were slushy and hard to drive on.

'We'll go by your old playgroup in a minute.'

As we travelled down the village street we could see that the Council had, as part of a rebuilding programme, at last demolished the house that had been home to both Jacqueline and me. The old village school behind the church was closed, its windows boarded up and slates missing from the roof. A rosy-faced girl with her little brother in hand was walking purposefully up School Lane. Is there still a Sunday School? She stared at us passing and did not know that we were not really outsiders.

So many of the children I grew up with, though I would scarcely recognize them now, still live in the village and now have children of their own. Theirs must be the boys who lounged against the school fence as we passed.

Some houses are tidier and smarter, others older and more dilapidated. The dirt was the same – messy clay that keeps every footpath mucky and slippery all through the winter and makes the puddles stand around for days after every shower.

We are all different now. We have all changed and some have moved. My elder sister now commutes to work in

London every day. My aunts and uncles have chosen this area for their retirement from noisier places on the edge of the city. When we arrived at my sister's house, several of our relatives were there, including two of my aunts, now retired. They had many questions about Jacqueline's plans for her future, for studying and a career.

While we were there, Jacqueline received a letter from an aunt and uncle of mine who had visited us in Hackney just after Jacqueline's birth. It reminded me of how welcome their visit had been.

Jacqueline is now an adult ready to launch into her own career, beginning work on a degree course. Our home is busy, both of us having many friends and interests. It is *our* home. I have certain parental responsibilities for what happens but I have chosen to share the responsibility of running the home and what it is like with Jacqueline.

Together we decide how to spend our money and what newspaper we want to read. Christmas celebrations are planned by both of us. This involves each of us recognizing the freedoms and responsibilities of the other and working out together how we want to live.

Recently someone asked me, 'Well, in your house do you let Jacqueline smoke?'

It is *our* house so this is a question we talk about together. If I am offended by the smoke, or I am choking on it, I can raise the question with Jacqueline. We may make a new decision or we may not. I am not the 'ultimate boss' in the home – I cannot tell Jacqueline to stop smoking; it is her decision.

I have chosen my set of life values; Jacqueline has set about the adult process of establishing her own, which may or may not differ from mine. When our values clash we have to talk and negotiate and find a workable solution.

We have talked about the fact that I should always try to make decisions together with Jacqueline, and aim never to go on with any plan that denies her rights as an adult

138

in our home. I try to respect her as a person. This does mean the onus is on her to decide whether or not she will respect me in the same way. While she was a child I required that of her; now she is an adult, I do not. It is her own choice.

Jacqueline is now a responsible and caring adult. I am no longer a parent in terms of having a protective role, or being responsible for what she does. We are very closely related and the future of our relationship depends neither on her dependence on me nor mine on her, but on whatever mutual respect and friendship we have as adults. Of course, I still worry about her and about other people, but her course in life is hers to determine.

Why should I want to curtail Jacqueline's freedom? For several years I have been aware that my life, my friendships and the kind of family life I want must not be dependent on Jacqueline's presence. It needs rather to be something constant which she can return to as she wants. So I have thought about what 'home' means and how it will be home when Jacqueline is away at college or finds a job somewhere else. It has been a matter of coming to terms now with my aloneness so that I do not use any other person to stop me feeling lonely. That has involved a spiritual discipline of awareness of God, of stillness and relaxation, of learning to deal creatively with my anxieties.

I am glad she is planning to go to university. I am glad she is succeeding in what she wants to do.

Jacqueline said a few days ago that she thought I had more determination than she has. I believe my sense of determination has grown out of the struggles I have gone through over the years. When it felt as if there was no option but defeat, it took great determination to begin to tackle those almost insuperable problems. I would like it not to be so hard for Jacqueline, but if the only way to discover determination is to live through adversity, then I would rather she followed it than not. I will offer encouragement and help, but not, I hope, any easy ways out.

Maybe my friendship can be of the quality I have found so helpful in others.

As I have tried to answer Jacqueline's questions about identity, and roles, over the years I have noticed something particular. I have started to uncover a system in which I see that women have only taken the lead through submissive stances. For hundreds of years women had no rights, except by their husband's permission, so they worked out how to use the most subtle means to get their own way. Most men do not even see it happening, because part of the woman's ploy is to get him to think it was his idea anyway! Other women can see it more readily. It is only as we have equal rights that we begin to free both men and women from this trap. But it may take a long time.

The last few years have assured me that Jacqueline is aware of her own potential as a person. More than anything else, this is what I wanted her to appreciate and understand about life and, by taking responsibility for herself, to realize her own value. This new generation she is in will achieve new things, make new inventions, discover new places. I could not train Jacqueline for them because I do not know what those new challenges will be or what skills are necessary. I could only offer a creative way of approaching challenge, creative problem-solving, not a set of answers.

I have now done the most weighty work of parenting. Jacqueline is an adult and many tasks are complete. She has been safe through years of dependency – moral, physical and social. She has gradually taken over the responsibility for herself. Sometimes my protection of her has not been too steady and my life choices have brought an outward appearance of insecurity. It is well known that single parents move house more than other families and I was no exception. But Jacqueline's emotional security saw her through these times.

In spiritual terms, Jacqueline has grown through all the stages of childhood and has now taken responsibility to make her own decisions. One day I sat in the library making notes about children's spiritual development and how parents can nurture and help them. The more I wrote, the more angry I got. I had done *all* these things, but Jacqueline was not conforming to my life's pattern for spirituality or faith.

I stopped writing and sat back. I asked God quite angrily, what good was it spending all these years to raise Jacqueline in all these worthwhile values in life if she was not conforming to what I wanted for her? If there was something else I had to do, why had I not found out before now?

It was then that I sensed God was saying, 'Jacqueline's and my relationship is no longer your business; leave it to us. We are quite able to work it ourselves.'

That reminds me of a story of a friend of mine, son of a priest, who, having grown up being very involved with his father's church, left home and went to college. Within weeks he had abandoned everything that his father stood for. He dreaded meeting his father again, feeling that his father would be disappointed.

Eventually he faced his father, and said, 'Dad, I have lost my faith.'

His father responded, 'No, you haven't. You have lost mine. Now you may be able to find your own.'

I will continue to help and encourage Jacqueline in appropriate ways as an adult. I enjoyed being Jacqueline's parent through her childhood. Given another chance, I might change some of my mistakes, but I do not regret the work it has been. I have so much enjoyed our friendship and what we have had in common that I am sure I would have been much poorer without it. I would have enjoyed spending more time with her.

Life with Jacqueline has opened my eyes to joys that I never would have appreciated otherwise. At times when it was hard work, Jacqueline's laughter caused me to look up and see more than I was feeling at the time. Her joy and sense of wonder re-awakened those same responses in me. Most recently, as Jacqueline has become more aware of her own potential, I have realized how much more I have still untapped in me.

Maybe parents who are physically old by the time their children leave home think of parenting as their life's work, especially mothers. But I am not yet forty and I have a whole lifetime in front of me, a slate and a chalk in hand. What shall I draw? What shall I become? I have discovered some of my potential through being a parent and time I have given to that. Now I want to go as far as I can in as many meaningful directions as I can.

I see, in Jacqueline, a repeat of some of my weaknesses in the next generation. I am very organized but untidy. While I see Jacqueline getting her life in order with regard to her choice of studies, her papers and books are all over the house. I very easily feel rejected and Jacqueline likewise has had to fight to get beyond feeling the same. Occasionally I have felt overwhelmed by my own imperfections and the way they have affected Jacqueline, but I am able to conclude that on the whole life has been good to us and our weaknesses can be forgiven.

The last few steps of being a single parent with an only child have taught me a great deal. It would be very easy to want to control Jacqueline, to trim her wings, so that I could determine that she stays at home with me! If she were passive, unmotivated and unadventurous, I could have kept her under my control and we could continue as parent and child. Thank God she is not! Her adventurous spirit may take her far from here but I would not want her to be any different. The freedom and excitement she feels about life and the obvious richness she finds in it I would never want to curtail.

The joy of my life is friendship. All friendships come and

go, ebb and flow, so I have to learn to relax and enjoy the friends of today. In this way I can be content in being alone or with others.

Now I look back and I look forward as a parent and as a single parent. I remember the struggles that might have been easier with a partner. There were good things, too. Would I change my life if I could do it again? Would I change my single parenthood to shared parenthood? Our life has been good. Out of the despair and bewilderment of the beginning has come a quality of life that might not otherwise have happened. Without having been so near dying, to giving up on life, would I enjoy life so much? If I had not had to deal with death, I might never have made a relationship with God. Would I ever have noticed his intervention in my life? Would I ever have noticed that the whole of life is his creation?

I have had no personal experience of 'shared' parenting, but my impression is that it reduces the weight of the responsibility and I would have been glad of that. At the same time, perhaps it is harder and more time-consuming for two people to make decisions than one. 'There are no clashing ideas or different opinions with one,' one father said to me.

If anyone finds themselves a single parent, it is possible to make a good job of it, though the amount of hard work involved makes me think I might not recommend it. Part of my confidence, I know, comes from my faith and having realized that life is a stream which I can harness and make something of creatively. As long as I was a single parent who felt crushed and overwhelmed there was no hope that I could be a good parent alone.

The hope I have, and the ray of hope I see, is not that life worked for us because of great miracles – or even little ones. It is that, among the ordinary circumstances of life, among good friends, a single parent can make it!

Just after we joined the Community of Celebration, my

parents and my sister's family came over for the day to see our new home and meet all our friends. We had a splendid lunch together in our household, then walked around the grounds. Jacqueline showed them round everywhere, introducing them to all the children. Later my mother said, 'Dad and I were talking about how much we like your new home. We enjoyed visiting you. What we realized is that you will probably never be rich, but you will be happy, and that is more important.'

Now Jacqueline is an adult, we have challenging conversations on a variety of topics. She introduces me to authors I ought to have known about. My own adult experience had dulled my awareness of questions about the meaning of life, or relationships and prejudices. I enjoy the fact that Jacqueline challenges my complacent attitudes and makes me more alert. My experience of life may be a certain asset to me, but I certainly need this breath of fresh air to blow away the cobwebs and make me look at life expectantly. So I am re-learning to be adventurous, to travel and have hopes and dreams for the future.

I sat on the Inter-City train as it racketed at high speed away from London. It banged and clattered so hard I could not read any more. I looked out of the window at the passing fields. The winter rain had stopped and the sun, though watery, was making a good show of setting. Even the dried and weather-bleached grasses, tattered and broken, were touched with colour. I watched till the sky was inky blue behind the lights of Christchurch. Happiness for our family has not been in laughter alone, for alone it would have become empty. Now we are happy because we have laughed and cried. We have seen new horizons and unclimbed mountains and found them to be reachable though hard, hard work. It has been worth it.

The story of my single parenthood is also the story of my Christian faith. The faith was what I found among the ashes of my breakdown, in the wake of emotional and

144

financial hardship. The problems, ordinary everyday problems, helped me discover that Christianity is faith in God who gave us ordinary human life to enjoy and make the most of, through all its ups and downs. My faith and my life are thoroughly wedded together. My faith has led me into living my everyday life much more fully. Since I have found that the hard times we go through are often the most creative, I would not want God to remove them and leave us with a bland Utopia. The difference afterwards between defeat and a good adventure is often only in how you get through it! Maybe suffering has some use to us.

What then of my days of despair? Do I wallow in them in a kind of emotional masochism? Winter seems to me to be a time of death and gloom – even the trees feel my despair, they are lank and dreary. On a wet day there is no escape from its chillness and the fire in the grate will not burn properly. The windows rattle and the draughts make the curtains shiver a little.

Only yesterday I saw a robin perched in the hedge, singing with all his heart, his red breast puffed out with the effort of singing and keeping warm. Beneath him in the flower border were the green spears of the daffodils, now several inches high, and one had a bud just forming. My days of despair pass like the winter. I wait for warmer times – for laughter, to feel good again, for fetes and sunshine, for flowers and fruit from the garden. Pain and sorrow were harder to bear when I saw them to be enemies. Both winter and sorrow are eventually followed by laughter and summer. So I will wait.

Appendix

If you are aware that you will soon become a single parent because you are single and pregnant or because you and your partner are working out a separation, go through all the items in this appendix. If you realize that you will need practical help, contact the various departments and organizations now, so that you begin single parenthood as securely as possible. At the very least this will result in your children feeling more secure.

Not everyone knows in advance: single parenthood often begins with a traumatic and unexpected event, a death or a spouse leaving without warning.

If you have young children or are expecting a baby, your **Health Visitor**, normally attached to the local doctor's practice, will be able to help you find the right people and places to contact. My own experience is not the norm, Health Visitors are really exceptionally helpful! If you move house, ask the local clinic to put you in touch with the Health Visitor in the new area.

Your local **Doctor** probably has a list of local help organizations and departments. He or she will be aware that you may be asking for Valium for your emotional state but that the practical problems require something else. Ask when you visit the surgery.

The **Citizens Advice Bureau** will have information on all kinds of help, voluntary and statutory. Finding practical ways to make life stable for you and your children is essential and the CAB will advise you on how to begin.

Many larger towns have councils of voluntary service; their knowledge of voluntary organizations and self-help groups in the area is excellent. Look them up in the Public Library.

The **Department of Health and Social Security** (**DHSS**) has lots of information on statutory rights and sources of help. The details are often very complicated and you may find you need help in sorting out what you should be claiming. The **Child Poverty Action Group** is probably the best source of information (they produce handbooks) and help in sorting out what you could be claiming from the DHSS, and non-means-tested benefits.

The crisis that results in a marriage breaking down often has its history in a series of accumulating problems that finally come to a head. The problems do not actually disappear when your partner goes, though some may be temporarily replaced by the crisis. Whatever the problems were that you and your partner were having, get help with them, for the sake of your children and your own future adult relationships. You may need personal counselling (Marriage Guidance); financial help and advice on money management; help with children's emotional or physical problems; or legal advice. Do not leave the situations untended for they will produce another crisis!

MONEY

Until you are sure of the financial stability of your family you will still be in a crisis stage of parenthood.

Using the agencies listed above, ask for all the information you can get and if the help you are offered does not meet your needs ask for advice on where else you should go for help. If in doubt contact the Child Poverty Action Group.

After being a single parent for eighteen years, I discovered that I could have been claiming Supplementary Benefit all those years! Why did I not claim the help in those early days when I most certainly needed it? Because I did not know it was there or that I was entitled to it. So while I am giving you some information on sources of financial help do ask at all the statutory and voluntary agencies for their advice.

The following state help is available:

• **Social Security payments** These are at set rates. While they are very low, below the poverty line, they are sufficient to keep a family going. The amounts paid are calculated to include your specific housing costs, rates and other overheads as well as food and clothing. (It does not help with car, television or telephone costs.) Exceptional expenses for which you need extra help in the form of a lump sum may be paid towards a new baby, clothes if you are pregnant, travel costs, starting work, a funeral, removal costs, some furniture, bedclothes, fuel, repairs, redecorating, rent in advance.

There is special Social Security help for one-parent families, so again check that you are receiving all that you are entitled to. Also there is extra Child Benefit for one-parent families.

• **Supplementary Benefit** is a source of help if your income is insufficient to meet your needs – for example, if you work part-time or for a low wage. You will be interviewed to assess the level of help to which you are entitled.

When you live off Social Security/Supplementary Benefit you may be able to work for several hours a week with only a minor effect on the payments you receive. Talk to the necessary department or to a social worker so you will not lose aid unnecessarily. For example, you will find it affirming to be out at a part-time job, mixing with other adults, but your child may go to a childminder or playgroup for which you pay. The amount you pay for your child's care may be deducted from your earnings before your Benefit is affected.

• **Family Income Supplement** is help for those who are earning, who are at work for more than twenty-four hours per week and are single parents. (Thirty hours if you are married.) The FIS is graduated according to how many children you have and is a payment made to bring your income up to a tolerable minimum.

If you qualify for any of the above payments you are additionally entitled to claim free school meals, free milk and vitamins, dental treatment, prescriptions and fares for hospital treatment.

The best source of information on the subject is *The National Welfare Benefits Handbook* by Janet Allbeson and John Douglas, published by the Child Poverty Action Group. Many voluntary organizations have this book for reference and it is often in the local library.

• **Maintenance money** awarded to you by a court or by agreement with your spouse, may be an additional source of income. It is seldom on its own enough for you to live on. If payments become intermittent talk to the Social Security Department, as payments can be made direct to them, ensuring that you get your money regularly. This can remove the awful anxiety of whether any maintenance will be paid. Your solicitor will be very helpful in telling you how to get maintenance on a reasonable and agreed basis.

LEGAL AID AND SOLICITORS
There is a lot of legal help available to you.

Look in the Yellow Pages or ask the local Citizens Advice Bureau. Make an initial inquiry about what aid is available and ask what expense is likely.

It is possible under 'the green form scheme' to get £40 initial help before a Legal Aid request is processed. Ask your solicitor to tell you about this scheme.

Your solicitor will advise you on the legal steps necessary for maintenance settlement, custody of children, separation and divorce, making a will, changing your name and other aspects of family affairs.

HOUSING

The first thing to know is that housing can be complicated!
Contact the Citizens Advice Bureau before taking action
if at all possible; some actions may result in your not
qualifying for statutory help. For example, in my area of
the country if you move into a holiday flat temporarily
you are considered voluntarily homeless and do not qualify
for emergency help.

However, anyone on Supplementary Benefit qualifies
for Housing Benefit. If you are renting privately-owned
housing, rent and rates will be paid in full. Council rents
and rates will be paid direct. If you are buying your own
home, your rates will be paid and the DHSS will pay the
interest on your mortgage under normal circumstances.
Make inquiries.

Make emergency inquiries with the Social Services if
violence means you must move immediately from the house
you have shared with your partner.

Many people are afraid of the old system where children
were taken into care if the family were homeless. That
system has gone. Children are never separated from their
parent because of homelessness, only if the children are
at risk because the parent is actually incapable of looking
after them. So do not be afraid to register as homeless and
ask for housing help.

SELF-HELP GROUPS

There are a number of different self-help groups around
the country. The **local library** or **CAB** will have a list of
all the local groups and will tell you of those that are for
single parents.

Experiences vary. Some people enjoy self-help groups
and find them helpful. That may be partly a result of their
own personality and partly because of the group – which
can change according to the personalities of the members
in it.

Unless the group has a well-kept rule against gossip, be careful what you say in group sessions.

My own experience of meeting men who think that I must be interested in an affair with them does happen sometimes in the context of these groups. When members are feeling lonely and discouraged and short of self-esteem they may well instinctively look for another marriage relationship to make them feel better. So do not be too shocked.

Many people are helped by self-help groups over the transition into single parenthood and in an ongoing way with child-care arrangements.

VOLUNTARY ORGANIZATIONS

The National Council for One-Parent Families will direct you to help as well as advising you on legal and housing matters. They will act on your behalf in some circumstances.

The Child Poverty Action Group are very helpful in looking at rights and benefits for families. Their leaflets and books give the most up-to-date and comprehensive list of information. If you are confused about your rights, they will help you.

In many areas the **Diocesan Council for Social Responsibility** normally found at Church House, usually in the Cathedral Close of each diocese, will also refer you to the best sources of help.

PROVISION FOR CHILDREN

Most areas have lists in the library, the Clinic and at the CAB.

For under-fives you will find a comprehensive list of toddlers groups, playgroups, nursery schools, day-care centres. Check whether child-minders are registered with the local authority, who will ensure good standards of care are maintained.

Many areas of the country now have supervised Holiday Play Schemes, so even during the school holidays your children have somewhere to go while you are at work.

ADDRESSES

National Council for One-Parent Families
255 Kentish Town Road, London NW5 2LX

Child Poverty Action Group
1 Macklin Street, London WC2B 5NH

Cruse (for the widowed)
126 Sheen Road, Richmond, Surrey

Gingerbread
Head Office, 9 Poland Street, London W1

Mothers in Action
9 Poland Street, London W1

National Council for Divorced and Separated
13 High Street, Little Shelford, Cambridge

FOR READERS IN AUSTRALIA

Salvo Care Line,
PO Box A688, Sydney South, NSW 2001
Phone: 683 4000

Anglican Counselling Centre
491 Kent Street, Sydney, NSW 2000
Phone: 267 3214

Life Line
210 Pitt Street, Sydney, NSW
Phone: 264 2222

Lone Parent Family Support Service
Cromer Community Centre, Fisher Road North,
Cromer, NSW
Phone: 982 5500

Parents Without Partners (Aust) Inc.
National Secretary,
PO Box 221,
Alderley, QLD 4951

Branches:
PWP (ACT) PO Box 465,
Dickson, ACT 2601

PWP (Tasmania) PO 115, Ulverstone,
TAS 7315

PWP (Nth T) PO 4290, Darwin, NT 5794

PWP (WA) Textile House, 504 Hay Street,
Perth, WA 6000

PWP (Qld) PO 164, Mater Hill Sth., Brisbane,
QLD 4101

PWP (SA) 1st Floor Steamship Building,
26 Currie Street, Adelaide, SA 5000

PWP (Vic) PO 21, Canterbury, VIC 3126

PWP (NSW) PO Box 277, Granville, NSW 2142